'Emily Wilson's brilliant reconsiderations of the ancient world – through the figure of Helen of Troy, the remaking of the *Iliad* by Christopher Logue, the use of comedy to grapple with dark matters, even slavery, and much besides – makes this an enthralling and profoundly relevant book'

Salman Rushdie

'I adored reading these joyful, illuminating and engrossing journeys through ancient literature. With wit, passion and clarity, she invites us into each of these fascinating subjects. The final essay especially is required reading for anyone interested in translation, drawing back the veil on how a brilliant scholar and writer approaches her work'

Madeline Miller

'Emily Wilson unlocks the gates to ancient Greece and Rome: her deep understanding of translation is the key'

Peter Stothard

'By turns witty, stylish, ethical and pugilistic, Wilson reveals herself to be as brilliant an essayist as she is a translator'

Tim Whitmarsh

'Wilson has produced a passionately personal – and at times polemic – celebration of language and the power of literature to speak across millennia'

David Stuttard

'Vaulting from the ancient to the modern and back again, this collection is erudite, insightful and provocative. An unparalleled insight into the work of a classicist and translator at the height of their powers'

Paul Cooper

'We're incredibly lucky to have Emily Wilson writing about the art, politics and ethics of translation and retranslation. *Crossing the Wine-Dark Sea* is an impressive display of Wilson's expertise, conviction and wit'

Jen Calleja

CROSSING THE WINE-DARK SEA

Journeys through Ancient Literature

EMILY WILSON

Profile Books

LRB

First published in Great Britain in 2026 by
Profile Books Ltd
29 Cloth Fair
London
EC1A 7JQ
www.profilebooks.com

and

London Review of Books
28 Little Russell Street
London
WC1A 2HN
www.lrb.co.uk

'Chill Out with the Stoics' (2010), 'The Trouble With Speeches' (2013) and 'Slut-Shaming Helen of Troy' (2014) previously published in the *New Republic*
'Web of Rome' previously published in the *TLS* (2016)
'War Music' previously published in *Translation and Literature* Vol. 25, Issue 3 (2016)
'The Pleasures of Translation' previously published in the *New York Review of Books* (2018)
'Ancient Worlds: Edith Hamilton and the Popularisation of the Classics' previously published in the *Nation* (2023)

5 7 9 10 8 6

Typeset in Dante by CC Book Production

Printed and bound in Great Britain by
CPI Group (UK) Ltd, Croydon, CR0 4YY

A CIP catalogue record for this book is available from the British Library.

Our product safety representative in the EU is BGC Sustainability & Compliance,. 7 avenue du Général Leclerc, Paris, 75014, France https://baldwinglobalconsulting.com

ISBN 978 1 80522 585 0
eISBN 978 1 80522 586 7

FSC
www.fsc.org
MIX
Paper | Supporting responsible forestry
FSC® C013604

For my sister Bee Wilson,
a brilliant writer and contributor to the *LRB*.
Sisters by chance, friends by choice.

CONTENTS

INTRODUCTION

In his wonderful long poem *Autumn Journal*, written on the eve of the Second World War, Louis MacNeice meditates on the value of looking back to Greek and Roman antiquity in such dark times – or, perhaps, at the futility of such an endeavour.

> And how one can imagine oneself among them
>   I do not know.
> It was all so unimaginably different
>   and all so long ago.

The lines gain their memorable heft from the surprising recurrence of 'imagine' in the long, emphatic word, 'unimaginably'. 'These dead are dead', the narrator insists – and so long gone that even to imagine them is perhaps impossible.

And yet, in this very same passage, MacNeice does imagine them. He dismisses the usual pieties and clichés in the version of 'classics' that was and is still taught in schools and colleges around the world: 'The Glory that was Greece; put it in a syllabus, grade it / Page by page / To train the mind or even to point a moral / For the present age'. MacNeice was himself a lecturer in classics, and his poem is preoccupied by the difference between fully, viscerally imagining the ancient world, and teaching it within the constraints of the existing educational system, as well as the prejudices and idealisations through which we often view the ancient Greek and Roman past. But there are elements of the ancient world that this twentieth-century poet can imagine all too clearly: 'the crooks, the adventurers, the opportunists ... I think of the slaves'. Daily life was very different in ancient times, as the speaker reminds us. Their customs are strange to us ('the women pouring / libations over graves'), and the paraphernalia of English university life in the 1930s would be strange to them ('Lifebuoy soap and muddy flannels ... chalk and ink and rows of pegs and lockers'). And yet those crooks, those adventurers, the human mess and muddle of 'truisms and humour' present across ancient literature – none of that is so very distant to the world we moderns know.

Translation provides the most intense test of the questions MacNeice raises: how can we imagine the ancients, in all their strangeness and all their strange familiarity? Or was it 'so long ago' that the task is impossible? How can we read their surviving words without projecting onto these texts false ideas – such as the notion that they must be edifying, a model of logic and luicidity? How can we see them instead as the creations of once-living, complex human beings? Can their words be brought back to life in a new language – or must the dead stay dead?

It is particularly difficult to create an experience like that of sung choral lyric in a paper-and-ink book, or to find modern equivalents for ancient obscenities and ancient scenes of comic violence, given the gaps between ancient and modern social values, or to reconstruct the emotional and stylistic effects of ancient drama and epic – which were, like archaic Greek lyric, originally designed for oral performance. Many modern translators have responded to these challenges by largely ignoring them, and rendering the musical rhythms of ancient metrical verse into English free verse or prose. This approach certainly makes the translator's task easier, and may seem to make things easier also for the reader. And yet it is, as I argue in this book, a debatable and costly choice: unmetrical translations of metrical verse do not convey the artfulness of the originals, which is a major component of their strangeness for a modern reader. Whenever possible, translators need to recreate not only the semantic meaning of ancient poetry, but also its formal qualities, such as metre and sound – even in a language whose sounds are, inevitably, entirely different. Language is never a neutral tool by which we represent the world: every word and phrase carries with it a tangle of cultural assumptions and connotations, many of which are not paralleled by other languages – especially languages from many centuries ago. Form is not entirely distinct from meaning, and aesthetics are always entangled with values.

In discussing both translation and the reception of ancient literature and ancient myth more broadly, I show how modern culture shapes contemporary responses to antiquity. As our world changes, we begin to see new shapes in the ever-shifting and murky waters of the past. A reorientation back to ancient literature – through translation or imitation or other kinds of deep engagement – can transform modern cultures for the better. Antiquity, in its strangeness and difficulty, can be radical. Modern readers, interpreters and translators can choose to assimilate the past to the present. But we can also choose to open ourselves to the surprise of the past, and allow it to change us.

The term 'antiquity' implies an enormous monolith, one that stands in contrast to 'modernity'. But it is crucial to disambiguate one strand of 'antiquity' from another. There are gaps that span centuries and hundreds of miles between archaic, classical Greek, and Roman cultures, and between the Roman Republic and the Roman Empire.

In several chapters – including those on Roman comedy, Aeschylus and Helen of Troy – I discuss ancient social hierarchies along lines of enslavement, class and gender. Most surviving ancient poetry was composed by men, usually men of an elite social class; representations of women and enslaved people in these texts tells us a great deal about how people in these categories may have been imagined, but very little about their own lived experiences. I also discuss tropes and ideas that were claimed by people from very different walks of life – such as Stoicism, a philosophical school favoured both by an emperor, Marcus Aurelius, and a former slave, Epictetus.

I trace the complex combination of chance, changing tastes and wilful editorialisation that led us to the canon of ancient literature that we have today. Many still-extant ancient authors were far more widely read in earlier eras than they are today. This applies to scientific writers such as the medical authority, Galen, who was once regarded as an invaluable source for cutting-edge advice on human antatomy, but whose work is interesting now for the history of science. The same is true for philosophical and conceptual writing: in the twenty-first century, Stoicism is particularly popular, while other ancient ethical schools, such as Epicureanism, are less so. Shifting canons also shape the receptions of more obviously literary texts, which can gain and lose popularity as modern cultural norms and interests change. Early modern readers were far more interested in Euripides' *Hecuba* than in his *Trojan Women* – whereas in the twentieth and twenty-first centuries, audiences and readers have favoured the theatrical representation of collective grief over the bloody revenge drama. Modern preferences, preoccupations and assumptions affect not only how we read ancient literature, but which elements of the past we choose to read and remember.

This book does not cover every possible extant text, author or period in ancient Greek and Roman literature with encyclopaedic thoroughness – a task that would be challenging even at three times the length. Rather, I aim to provide an engaging and accessible introduction to some central themes within the interpretation and translation of ancient literature and its relationship to modernity. Many of the pieces here began life as reviews, written at various times over the past twenty years. All have been thoroughly revised and reworked, and organised to serve as stand-alone introductions to a number of canonical works of ancient Greek and Roman literature, and to central issues in the reception and translation of ancient culture in the twenty-first century.

I begin with a case study of the modern translation and reception of the archaic Greek lyric poet, Sappho. This example allows me to lay out two central themes: the challenges of reimagining ancient literary forms for new cultural contexts, and the intersections between modern norms and the receptions of antiquity. I explore the gaps between the musical, choral performance genre of archaic Greek lyric – so different from our textual, digital notions of 'lyric' poetry – and between ancient and modern ideas about gender and sexuality. From there, I move to a broader discussion of literary translation, including some consideration of changing norms of translation practices, and the history of translation studies. The third essay moves back to antiquity and charts the central role of translation, showing how Roman literary culture was founded on the translation and creative imitation of the Greeks.

The next two essays explore the relationships between ancient and modern cultural assumptions more broadly. One piece considers ancient political uses of rhetoric, and the uses of stylish, memorable language to distort historical and economic truth. The other focuses on continuities and differences between ancient and modern forms of misogyny, concentrating on the mythical figure of Helen, the cunning, perceptive, half-divine woman whose abduction by Paris precipitated the Trojan War – and who becomes, after antiquity, known primarily for her looks, not her intelligence.

In the next trio of essays, I discuss gender and politics from a different angle, examining how ancient Greek and Roman norms of masculinity, sexuality and the proper uses of power differ from those of modern cultures. This cluster of topics is particularly pressing for translators of ancient comic literature, because it is so often obscene – and yet the boundaries of what is just shocking enough to be funny, but not so horrifying as to be unfunny, are radically different from one culture to another. Ancient humour often hinges on jokes that rely on alien notions of 'proper' sexuality or 'proper' masculine identity, and on the supposedly humorous potential of violence and humiliation directed against enslaved people – jokes that are less likely to land well with a modern reader or audience. I discuss these issues in three essays on Greek comedy, Roman comedy, and the playful, aggressive, sometimes comic Roman poet Catullus. I suggest that it is particularly challenging for modern translators to find equivalents for texts that are both deliberately indelicate and artfully poetic, and to translate jokes that depend on the normalisation of social structures that modern readers may find bizarre, like the idea that performing oral sex is inherently degrading, or morally abhorrent, like slavery.

Comic genres often profess to offer only entertainment, not instruction. And yet humour frequently does provide a kind of cultural education in what a society finds shocking or acceptable. I turn next to the much more explicitly didactic genre of ancient philosophical teaching, focusing on the writings of the Stoic teacher, Epictetus, with a glance ahead to Marcus Aurelius. I show that the modern popularity of adapted forms of ancient Stoicism speaks to a particular set of parallels between our time and that of the Roman Empire as times of turbulence and uncertainty, including for the most powerful members of society.

I then turn back to ancient Greek literature, to examine how the most elevated and highly valued genres of poetry in antiquity, epic and tragedy, articulate both social and literary values that only partly overlap with those we may find familiar. I consider what the performance poetry of Homer and Aeschylus might have been saying in its own time, and the challenges – for poets as well as translators – in bringing this poetry to life in a new era. I discuss the limitations of 'literal' approaches to translating ancient poetics, and what is gained and lost in livelier, more creative modes of interpretation. I interweave my discussion of translation with consideration of how modern attitudes towards gender, violence, poetics, power and truth may impact and limit our abilities to imagine or reimagine these ancient works.

Returning to modernity, I consider the state of popular receptions of ancient literature in the twentieth and twenty-first century. I discuss the extraordinarily successful and influential work of Edith Hamilton, and of the bestselling modern British and American translations of the Homeric poems. I suggest that the specific values of modern anglophone readers, especially a tendency to idealise 'greatness' and an individualistic model of freedom, have had a large impact on modern translations, receptions and perceptions of the ancient world and its literary remains. I argue that the classical scholars, translators, teachers and popularisers of the future need to nurture the skill of writing as well as close reading, and think broadly and deeply about how we might not merely replicate familiar ways of imagining ancient literature, but imagine it anew.

In the final piece, I comb closely through the translatorly choices of several different translators of Homer, showing how each responds differently to the original, or, in some cases, how translators may copy one another, and fail to take the opportunity to rethink the original. I emphasise the need for translators and others to embrace the possibilities afforded by the clash of languages, ancient and modern, and by the rich, confusing conflict between antiquity and our own time. I end with a brief afterword, in which I lay out a set of twenty principles that guide my own practice as a translator of ancient literature.

I hope this book will interest readers who may have no previous familiarity with ancient literature, as well as some who do. Times are always a-changing; but the twenty-first-century world is changing at an extraordinarily rapid pace – technologically, politically, culturally, economically and environmentally. Even the past of ten years ago – before Covid, before Brexit, before Trump, before the advent of ChatGPT, before the devastating wars in Ukraine and Gaza – can feel 'unimaginably different' from the present moment. It is easy to be swept up in the intense changes and anxieties of each new day. But in an era of so many dizzying transformations, it is more valuable than ever to remember that the world has not always been as it is now, nor as it was ten or even a hundred years ago. A turn back to ancient Greek and Roman cultures reminds us that the crooks and adventurers have always been with us, and also that cultural norms and literary traditions have changed radically, sometimes in ways that are difficult to see without a close reading of both the ancient past and the contemporary present. A turn back to imagine the unimaginable world of antiquity can help us understand and reimagine our own rapidly changing society.

Moreover, now that artificial intelligence threatens to take over our classrooms, our reading, our writing and our minds, it is useful to pay ever-closer attention to language, and to consider the power of words, to persuade, instruct and entertain. The dead are dead, and yet some of their words remain. In reading the few scraps of literature that survive from the ancient past, and in considering the words chosen to translate and retranslate them for each new generation of readers, we see how language shapes and is shaped by shifting human cultures and human choices. The juxtaposition of ancient and modern languages, literatures and lives reminds us that it is through our words that we are remembered and understood, long after our deaths, and that even the most minute differences of language or phrasing may make all the difference. Language writes us, but we, too, have the power to change the world by changing our words.

TONGUE BREAKS

Sometime around the ninth century CE, Sappho's nine books were irrecoverably lost. We have some tantalising scraps, single lines and short quotations, but only one complete poem – the wonderful 'Ode to Aphrodite' (Fragment 1), which is quoted in its entirety by Dionysius of Halicarnassus. A few long passages from other poems have been preserved in other authors: the most famous is Fragment 31 ('He seems to me equal to gods'), quoted at length in *On the Sublime* (a Greek work of literary criticism of unknown authorship, dating to about the first century CE). Until the end of the nineteenth century, these two poems were practically all that was known from the work of the poet Plato called 'The Tenth Muse'. Then, in the early 2000s, some scraps of papyrus from an ancient rubbish tip at Oxyrhynchus in Egypt turned out to contain fragments of poetry – including substantial chunks of Sophocles, Euripides and Sappho. In 2004, the broken corpus was augmented by an important new discovery from papyrus: a very substantial passage from a poem about Tithonus and the experience of old age. In 2014, more 'new Sappho' came to light, on papyri acquired illegally by the now disgraced papyrologist, Dirk Obbink – at the time, a faculty member at Oxford, who allegedly stole over a hundred papyrus fragments from the Egyptian Exploration Society, and sold several stolen biblical papyri around 2010 for large sums of money. Under these circumstances, the provenance of the second 'new Sappho' is morally and legally questionable, and some scholars have even questioned whether the Obbink finds are really Sappho at all. These papyri included a large chunk of the so-called 'Brothers' poem, in which the narrator addresses her two named siblings. But even with these additions, we have only a tiny percentage of the poet's oeuvre. Reconstructing Sappho from what remains is still like trying to get a sense of a whole Tyrannosaurus rex from one claw.

Both scholars and creative writers have made much of Sappho's fragmentariness. Anne Carson's translations, with facing Greek text, make effective use of blank space and brackets to convey the feeling of a torn or burned scrap of papyrus. Carson, whose translation was created too soon to include any of the 'new' Sappho poems, loves the spaces almost as much as the words: she says in her introduction that 'brackets imply a free space of imaginal adventure'. Here, for instance, is Fragment 24D:

]
]
]
]
]
] in a thin voice
]

The four words of Carson's poem are a haunting translation of a single word in Greek: *leptophon*.

Carson provides brief but useful notes to help even the Greekless reader to understand some of the textual problems in Sappho. She tries to translate nothing that is not in the Greek, and to follow the original word order and line breaks as far as possible. Here is her version of Fragment 31:

> He seems to me equal to the gods that man
> whoever he is who opposite you
> sits and listens close
> to your sweet speaking
> and lovely laughing – oh it
> puts the heart in my chest on wings
> for when I look at you, even a moment, no speaking
> is left in me
> no: tongue breaks and thin
> fire is racing under skin
> and in eyes no sight and drumming
> fills ears
> and cold sweat holds me and shaking
> grips me all, greener than grass
> I am and dead – or almost
> I seem to me.
> But all is to be dared, because even a person of
> poverty

And there the text breaks off. The great thing about this translation is its poverty. Unlike other translators, Carson adds no possessive pronouns or definite articles that are not present in the Greek. Sappho's speaker can no longer recognise her tongue as 'my' tongue; her eyes and ears and skin are no longer her own.

Carson is also aware that repetition matters. Sappho's own inability to speak ('no speaking') is mocked by the echo of her beloved's 'sweet speaking'. In Carson's version, as in the Greek, the first line and the penultimate line parallel one another ('He seems to me ... I seem to me'). The lover disintegrates as she contemplates the beloved object, until she can no longer speak or see or hear. But the controlling perceptions of the poet (the 'me' to whom it all 'seems') shape the narrative of the poem. The tension between the self who desires and the self who notices, often fudged in translation, has been an essential element in the influence of Sappho's poem on later writers of lyric.

For Carson, Sappho's gender and sexual orientation are of relatively little interest. But Sappho's words themselves are not gender-neutral. Carson's translation of Fragment 31 does not make clear what is clear in the Greek: that the beloved and the first-person speaker are both female. When it is necessary for the translator to make a choice about gender, Carson chooses to reduce or eliminate the possibilities of same-sex desire in Sappho. For instance, Sappho 102 expresses overwhelming longing for a *pais*, which could mean either a boy or a girl; Carson makes it 'boy'.

Carson's earlier book-length essay about desire, *Eros the Bittersweet*, figured prominently on the television series *The L Word*. But this popular vision of a lesbian or lesbian-friendly

Carson owes more to projection than to close reading. The 'queerness' of Carson's reimagining of Sappho lies primarily in its quasi-modernist or avant-garde style, with its focus on abstraction and the aestheticisation of the fragmentary – an oddly old-fashioned mode for the early twenty-first century. In a normal scholarly edition of a fragmentary ancient text, the editor provides a wide array of information about the missing elements, including specifying clearly which 'fragments' are quotations from other ancient authors, which are from torn pieces of papyrus, which words are illegible or supplied by scholarly conjecture, and what partial words or letters might be legible to provide clues about the missing elements. Carson offers some information about sources in her notes at the back, but in the main text the absences are marked by undifferentiated square brackets. The gaps and omissions in the text are presented as an aesthetic object rather than as evidence of the transmission of the lost originals. After the publication of her Sappho translation, Carson collaborated with her husband, the installation artist Robert Currie, to create a show in which some performers raise their arms into square brackets to mark the typography while others read the translations. The piece is enjoyably silly, and very much in keeping with the aesthetics of the 1960s avant-garde art scene; despite being created in the 2000s, it has a charming air of anachronism. Carson's range of interests – in visual and performance art as well as poetry – and her artful, mournful, often funny lyrical modes of expression are in tune with several musicians of her generation, including David Byrne and David Bowie. One might think the play with typography takes us a rather long way from the primarily sonic, musical, choral poetry of Sappho herself. But one could also argue that Carson's piece restores the performative aspects of ancient choral lyric, substituting the visual ornaments of blank space, and moving arms for the lost glories of Sappho's music, and the lost sound of ancient tapping feet.

Carson's career has always been about blurring the boundaries between classical scholarship and imaginative practice. Trained in art and design as well as ancient Greek and Latin, Carson is a prolific creator of work that is often difficult or impossible to put into traditional generic boxes. Often, these gaps are the point. Her deep engagement with ancient literature is constantly interwoven with themes and ideas drawn from her own life and experience, and vice versa. She loves to slip between the personal, the historical and the general, and between whimsical humour and dark horror. In her numerous versions of ancient Greek tragedy, Carson frequently inserts anachronistic references and creative riffs on the original, to greater or lesser degrees in different works. Often, these variations and departures will be invisible or inaudible to someone who has not read the original. To take one example, in her *Elektra* the protagonist is made to say to her loathed mother, 'You are some sort of punishment cage / locked around my life.' It's a striking pair of English lines, but the memorable image of the locked 'punishment cage' is Carson's invention, with no antecedent in Sophocles.

By contrast, Carson's Sappho translations are much more

readily legible as 'translations' of the Greek, rather than loose riffs inspired by an ancient original. But all translations are shaped by the interests, training, interpretative frameworks and perspectives of their creators. Carson's Sappho invokes Aphrodite as the goddess 'of the spangled mind' (*poikilophron*, rather than an alternative ancient reading, *poikilothron*, which would mean 'of the spangled throne'), reflecting Carson's own interest in emotional, artistic and cognitive multiplicity. She has much to say about the intricacies of 'Sappho's mind', but nothing about her complicated status as an aristocrat in an era of political turbulence and revolution, and nothing about her composition of songs to be performed with musical accompaniment by a chorus of women.

The Sappho volume harmonises with Carson's abiding interest in a minimalist aesthetics, and in absence as a defining feature of experience. A running theme of her work has been the desire to cut words down to the knucklebone, to find the simplest, shortest way of telling the truth. Omissions – even those caused by the accidents of history – are taken to provide access to an inner or higher truth. As Carson's Canadian compatriot Leonard Cohen sings, 'There is a crack, a crack in everything / That's how the light gets in'. In her first book, *Eros the Bittersweet* – whose title is taken from Sappho's oxymoronic description of desire – Carson characteristically suggests that the experience of painful desire has always been defined by absence. Drawing on a startlingly broad range of texts from across cultural and literary history, Carson constantly flits between three distinct spheres of reality: the historical, the universal and the personal. If her account of desire as absence was clearly articulated as a claim about historical fact, a pedant like me might push back on various generalisations, omissions and distortions. For me personally, Carson's very abstract, very literary account of *eros* that often feels a long way from my own specific, complicated experiences of relationships with real-life, embodied human beings. But perhaps this, too, is to miss the point: Carson's work is best read not as an analysis, either of ancient literature or of human experience, but as a striking kind of performance art on the page: it seeks less to make a philosophical or critical argument, or even to reveal a personal, emotional truth, than to cast a kind of spell, one in which we can be momentarily held captive by a strange and original form of visual and verbal experience.

Lawrence Sterne's rollicking comic novel, *The Life and Opinions of Tristram Shandy*, includes a famous moment where the narrator invites the reader to imagine his own version of a beautiful woman, 'as unlike your wife as your conscience will let you', and provides a blank page into which the reader can project his fantasies. The deliberately blank spaces of Carson's version of Sappho offer some of the same zany invitations to readerly play. Just as Sterne's narrator suggests no particular pre-existing model for the beautiful woman, so Carson suggests that the reader need not worry too much about what Sappho herself originally composed or sang. Carson's version of the ancient poet is fascinatingly disembodied, except for her new, infinitely re-inscribable body on the blank page.

But what of real, historical Sappho, a poet who lived in a particular time and place, and whose experiences of desire – and of community, politics, wealth, birth, friendship, music, family and age – presumably informed her poetry? Perhaps such questions are not fully answerable. 'It seems that she knew and loved women as deeply as she did music', Carson remarks in her introduction to her Sappho translations. 'Can we leave the matter there?' The answer, of course, is no. Sappho is the first surviving female author in the ancient Greek tradition, and most of the critical and imaginative responses to her life and work have treated her gender and sexuality as the most important facts about her – although more recent scholarship has begun to think more expansively about the poet's cultural milieu.

'Sapphic' and 'lesbian' acquired their modern meanings only very recently. In classical Athens, the island of Lesbos was associated with sexual activity in general, but primarily with blow jobs. In Jeffrey Henderson's classic study of obscene language in Attic comedy, *The Maculate Muse* (1975), the index entry for 'Lesbianism' reads: 'See Fellatio'. The Greek verb *lesbiazein* means 'to fellate'. The island was known for other things as well, such as sweet wine and sweet music, but not for girl-on-girl action.

Until the end of the nineteenth century, the usual English terms for lesbian practices did not draw on classical literature. Women could be 'lovers of their own sex', or, in the more frank Greek loanword, 'tribades' (literally 'rubbers'; the words 'rubster' and 'fricatrice' were also used in the seventeenth century). The *OED* cites no usage of 'lesbianism' in the modern sense before 1870, when it was used to argue that Swinburne's obsessive interest in Sapphic love was just as 'loathsome' as sodomy.

The words matter. It was through Sappho that female homosexuality came to be understood as a distinct sexual orientation, and as a distinctly sexual set of practices. Sex between women was often not seen as sex, but as harmless touching and kissing. Sappho's poetry was a reminder that desire between women could be as intense as heterosexual desire. Certainly, pre-nineteenth-century versions of Sappho did not always keep her locked in the closet. Donne's wonderful verse epistle 'Sappho to Philaenis' is the first English poem to describe what Sappho did with her girlfriend. The term 'lesbian loves' was used in 1736, in a satirical attack on a group of learned ladies. Yet before the nineteenth century, Sappho's sexuality was far from clearly defined. Things changed when Théophile Gautier made tribadism a fashionable feature of French decadence, and Baudelaire reminded the world that it had all started on Lesbos. It is only a slight exaggeration to say that Baudelaire, through Sappho, invented modern lesbianism, and Swinburne brought it to England. Classicists in the late nineteenth century, protective of Hellenic purity, tried to repress Sappho's sexual orientation: Ulrich von Wilamowitz-Moellendorff fantasised that she ran a girls' school, which helped dispel the whiff of impropriety.

For ancient pundits, the problem with Sappho was her licentiousness, not her sexual orientation. In his *Letters to Lucilius*, the Roman writer and philosopher Seneca cites the question of 'whether Sappho was a prostitute' as an example of familiar time-wasting questions. Those who admired her poetry but disliked the idea of promiscuity found a simple solution: there must have been two Sapphos on the island of Lesbos, one a courtesan and the other a great poet.

According to ancient legend, Sappho was bisexual. After various affairs with girls, she supposedly fell in love with a ferryman called Phaon, and threw herself off the Leucadian Rock in order to rid herself of her passion. This influential story, which goes back at least as far as the Greek comic poet Menander in the fourth century BCE, was probably inspired by allusions in Sappho's poetry to an Adonis-like myth about the ageing Aphrodite and a young sun deity called Phaon (perhaps identifiable with Phaethon). The legend was widely known in post-classical times through an Ovidian or pseudo-Ovidian epistle, 'Sappho to Phaon', and assumed a central position in almost all later responses to the poet. Later writers often use the story of the Leucadian leap as a misogynistic fable, an emblem of the comeuppance awaiting any woman who is too intellectual and too highly sexed. Erica Jong's novel, *Sappho's Leap* (2003), corrects the legend by describing a Sappho who is unharmed by her various sexual adventures, which include an encounter with a younger lover called Phaon (presumably zipless, given the nature of ancient fashion). Jong's Sappho falls from the rock almost by accident, and is blessed with a happy ending – in defiance of the earlier tradition of a lesbian woman poet punished by her own inevitable heterosexuality.

Jong's novel is just one of a long line of works about Sappho by women writers. An early example is Mary Robinson's breathless sonnet sequence, *Sappho and Phaon* (1796). Robinson aspires to sublimity, but, sadly, her writing sounds like this:

> In vain you fly me! on the madd'ning main
> SAPPHO shall haunt thee 'mid the whirlwind's roar.

It is not surprising that women writers who are attracted to Sappho simply because they want to celebrate her gender should produce pretty turgid results. Unmitigated panegyric is seldom fun to read, and sentimentality, even vaguely feminist sentimentality, does not age well.

Furious ranting is often more enjoyable than gushing praise. Sylvia Plath's 'Lesbos' powerfully presents the island as an unreachable ideal place, the counterpart to everything that is wrong with real women's lives. The speaker and her beloved could meet on Lesbos, 'in another life', but 'Meanwhile there's a stink of fat and baby crap.' Jeanette Winterson's response to Sappho is even angrier. In *Art and Lies*, her Sappho cries in outraged capital letters: 'WHAT HAVE YOU DONE WITH MY POEMS?' In fact, the proportion of lost work is no higher for Sappho than for many other ancient poets. With the new papyrological discoveries, we have somewhat more of Sappho's work than survives from her fellow Lesbian poet, Alcaeus, who was in his time an equally important figure, and whose work had a great impact on Horace. But the damaged text of Alcaeus has no value as a political symbol, whereas the gaps in Sappho can be used as an image of male oppression. For Winterson, the loss of Sappho's poetry represents the damage done to women's bodies and women's writing by centuries of patriarchy.

Margaret Reynolds dedicates *The Sappho History* 'To Jeanette Winterson, with love', and declares that Winterson's fictional Sappho is the closest you can come to 'the real Sappho'. Like Winterson, Reynolds sees Sappho as an emblematic female artist, whose work has been mutilated by male writers, critics and scholars. She argues that both Baudelaire and Swinburne 'break up Sappho, dissect her, fragment her and insert themselves into her spaces'. By contrast, she claims, female writers have treated those blank spaces as an opportunity for sharing. In the nineteenth century a pair of women, lesbians in the modern sense and also aunt and niece, published a set of imitations of Sappho under the name 'Michael Field'. They achieve, Reynolds argues, a 'duet where Sappho is not a rival, but a partner'.

But this sentimental cluster of notions about women does not stand up to much scrutiny. It is not only men who mutilate texts. Almost all the Greek quoted in *The Sappho History* is garbled, and Reynolds gives a nonsensical account of Sappho's metre, Sapphics. This is upsetting, at least for anyone who cares about Sappho's actual poetry. Reynolds freely admits that she is not a classical scholar, and that her subject is not Sappho herself, nor the Greek text of Sappho's poems, but the work of later writers and artists who imitated and alluded to her. This leaves unanswered a pair of central questions in ancient reception studies. Can one adequately discuss the later translation and reinvention of an ancient text without being able to read it oneself? And, more broadly, do translators, artists, poets and scholars look back to antiquity as a mirror in which we always find ourselves, or to discover the alien cultural norms of that very different country, the past?

Reynolds enthusiastically and uncritically adopts a metaphor that is all too common in writing about Sappho: the poet's literal body is associated with the body of her text. It is but a skip to the further claim that appropriations of this female 'body' by male writers, such as Tennyson or Swinburne, must be seen as murder or rape. But textual bodies are not really much like human physical bodies. For one thing, the gender of texts is much more fluid than Reynolds allows, and not necessarily identical with the gender of the author or creator. Men do not always write as men, or women as women. It would be more plausible to say not that Tennyson murders or rapes Sappho, but that through her he discovers his own lesbian identity. Moreover, any successful poetic adaptation involves an alteration of the original. There is no reason to assume in advance that male poets are always metaphorically raping Sappho, while female poets sing with her.

For instance, the great late nineteenth-century Decadent poets, Baudelaire and Swinburne, both evoke a sense of deep identification with Sappho. In Baudelaire's 'Lesbos', the 'brutal man', Sappho's male lover Phaon, breaks the perfection of homoeroticism. For Baudelaire, as for Donne, the idea of two women in bed together seems like perfection.

Lesbianism promises a new kind of language as well as a new kind of sexuality: words and materiality will at last achieve total unity. The only place where the mirror cracks is in the account of Sappho's death. The stanza begins, '– De Sapho qui mourut le jour de son blasphème', and ends, non-identically, 'De celle qui mourut le jour de son blasphème'. Sappho's 'blasphemy' is her lapse into heterosexuality. She is killed by this aberrant moment. But the poem also suggests that the self stands somewhere outside the homo/hetero dichotomy. The one word not repeated is 'Sapho'. Like the figure of the poet elsewhere in Baudelaire, Sappho is unique, isolated and different.

Classicists have recently challenged the idea of Sappho as a poet of individual desire. Some speculate that her poetry created a cohesive social group for women, through their shared interests in sex, marriage and private life. Much of her work may have been performed with a chorus, rather than by a single singing voice (although then again, it may not have been; we don't really know). Feminist scholars try to find in Sappho a vision of language and desire based not on hierarchy, difference and distance, but on 'intersubjectivity' and mutuality.

But an unqualified emphasis on collectivity misses one of the most distinctive features of Sappho's poetry. Her work speaks to shared group experiences, and many of these poem-songs were presumably created to be performed at ritual celebrations, such as weddings and the transition of girls to womanhood (the latter celebrated with songs known as *partheneia*, from *parthenos*, 'unmarried girl'). And yet

Sappho often marks these group occasions by reflecting on individual isolation and loss – on the possibility of stepping outside the group, or being excluded from it. Fragment 31 articulates a feeling that belongs to all of us only insofar as we are all sometimes alienated both from others (the couple, the man who looks, the girl who laughs) and from ourselves. The self disintegrates as the speaker observes and catalogues her own contradictory symptoms, until 'tongue breaks' and she can no longer see or feel. Sappho's poems emphasise the isolation of the individual, even within the group and even from herself. Similarly, in the newly rediscovered Tithonus poem, the speaker laments her failing, ageing body, and her distance from younger women dancers. Isolation and fragmentation are important subjects in Sappho's poetry, not just what happened to her work. Sappho appealed to later poets because she created a new way of speaking about distance, alienation and desire. If her work is universal, it is not because she invites us in – even if 'we' belong to particular marginalised groups, as women, lesbians or oppressed minorities – but because she shows us what it means to be excluded and alone.

THE PLEASURES OF TRANSLATION

In 2016 the International Booker Prize was awarded for the first time to a single novel, *The Vegetarian*, which was translated from the Korean. The award was shared by its author, Han Kang, and its translator, Deborah Smith. Kang and Smith are friendly collaborators, and Smith has translated Kang's subsequent work. But the translation aroused controversy in late 2017 when Korean readers accused Smith of not knowing the language well enough to render it responsibly, supposedly producing an English version that is not really a 'translation' at all. Smith's English version was considered by some to be a betrayal of the original, despite the fact that the author seems to have been perfectly happy with it, and despite the acclaim it received. The literary storm revealed how fraught the entire topic of translation can be, and how little agreement there is about what exactly counts as a good translation.

The study of translation can be traced back to the Romans, if not before; Cicero, himself a practising translator from Greek poetry and philosophy, makes interesting and influential comments about the importance of translating 'sense for sense' not 'word for word'. Cicero's maxim was cited by Jerome against Augustine, and recalled again by

Ezra Pound against Vladimir Nabokov, each arguing for the need to translate 'sense for sense', rather than 'word for word'. Assumptions about 'correct' translation practices have changed according to different cultural and literary norms: for instance, in the eighteenth century it was entirely normal to translate ancient Greek and Roman verse, which never rhymes, into rhyming couplets, and to transliterate Greek names with their Roman equivalents (Odysseus became Ulysses, Zeus became Jupiter, and so on – to the bewilderment of many modern readers). The contemporaries of Dryden and Pope would have been baffled by the idea that ancient metrical verse could be translated without metre, because unmetrical 'free verse' did not yet exist in anglophone and European literary culture.

Modern assumptions about how to approach translation tend to vary depending on the genre of the original text, and its status in the receiving culture. Readers of contemporary fiction are likely to expect a 'good' translation to read smoothly and fluently in English, masking its status as a translation, whereas readers of canonical ancient literature in translation are less likely to have these expectations, no matter how smooth or fluent the original may be. The Greek and Hebrew Bible is an unusual and fascinating case because it is so often read in translation into multiple languages by people around the world, because so many people are passionately attached to incompatible opinions about 'correct' biblical translation, and because so many have died for getting it 'wrong'. The Bible is, therefore, a good test case for charting multiple ways that translations might respond to the original. The missionary Eugene A. Nida famously argued that a phrase such as 'white as snow' should be rendered, for a culture without snow, as 'white as egret feathers'. In the case of a holy text, varying theological positions result in very different translation practices. Luther's German-language translation of the New Testament (1522) was designed to provide the people with something more like direct access to the word of God. The 2021 translation by the classicist and Quaker Sarah Ruden invites readers to encounter the same text anew, as an alien work of a distant historical time.

In the contemporary English-speaking world, the discipline of translation studies took off as a distinct academic subject in the 1970s, after James Holmes, a translator of Dutch poetry into English, called for a new classification of the field in his article 'The Name and Nature of Translation Studies' (1972). Since then, many academics who are not themselves practising translators have built careers out of 'translation theory', while some translators promote theories that seem significantly at odds with their practice. As Mark Polizzotti points out in his 2018 polemic, *Sympathy for the Traitor*, the academic study of translation tends to involve 'increasingly abstract discourse', which is useless for helping people understand what translation is, and does nothing to enable the production of better translations – or even to help us define what 'better' or 'worse' might mean in this case.

The rise of translation theory is partly a response to the increase in courses in colleges and universities on literature read in translation. One of the earliest Great Books courses was developed at Columbia University in 1917–1919, as an explicit response to the First World War: the first element was a study of 'Contemporary Civilisation in the West', focusing on 'Peace Issues', supplemented from 1920 onwards with a second course focused on 'Masterworks of Western Literature'. Many more courses on Great Books or Western civilisation sprang up around the US. In later decades, the focus on Western literature came to seem limited and ideologically dubious. Paradoxically, a curriculum that had been designed in the early twentieth century with the explicit goal of warding off the threats of fascism and authoritarianism was soon claimed by those sympathetic to these very tendencies. More and more institutions began to offer courses in world literature or global literary studies. But whether focused on 'the west' or 'the world', translation is the bedrock of all these courses. Students and their teachers cannot be expected to learn all the languages in which the most canonical literary works of the world are written. Inevitably, all the non-anglophone books on the syllabus – the Koran, Homer, Tolstoy, *Sundiata*, Balzac, *The Tale of Genji* – are read in translation.

The centrality of translation to the study of world literature and comparative literature, at least at the undergraduate level and for the general reader, creates a particular set of mixed feelings. On the one hand, without translation, most of us would have little or no access to most of the literary wealth of the world. Translation allows us to cross linguistic boundaries and opens our eyes to entirely different cultural experiences and forms of literature. I feel deep gratitude to the translators who have enabled me to read Korean,

Japanese, Arabic, Hebrew, Sanskrit and Swedish literature, among others, given that I will not have time to learn any of these languages in the limited number of years I am likely to remain alive.

On the other hand, reading this diverse body of texts in English translation risks creating a false kind of homogeneity. Translators are often expected to make their work sound comfortingly familiar for readers of English-language novels, even if the traditions in which the originals were created are quite different. Literary categories familiar to most English speakers – the novel, tragedy, comedy, epic, lyric, or the sonnet – have their own specific histories, and are not universals that have existed in every literary culture. Moreover, English is a language of colonialism and empire, and translation can be seen as yet another tool by which English speakers impose their hegemony on the world and silence other voices. Emily Apter, in the provocatively titled *Against World Literature* (2013) and the earlier *The Translation Zone* (2005), has pointed to the dangers of the 'liberal inclusiveness' implied by the study of world literature in translation, and argued for a greater recognition of what might be untranslatable across literary and linguistic traditions.

Apter's qualms about the value and ideology of translation are in many ways characteristic of translation studies as a whole, which is, as Polizzotti suggests, 'one of the few disciplines in which the study of a subject seems bent on demonstrating that very subject's futility'. Two thinkers are revered by many contemporary translation theorists with something like spiritual devotion. The first is Friedrich

Schleiermacher (1768–1834), a German theologian often dubbed the father of modern hermeneutics, who argued for a 'foreignising' style of translation in order to educate and enrich the target language, in his case, German.

The second is the great German-Jewish intellectual Walter Benjamin, whose essay 'The Task of the Translator' (1923) drew on his mystical notion of 'pure language', the sum of all languages, which can supposedly be accessed when a foreign text is translated with such syntactical literalness as to convey not its meaning, but its 'mode of signification'. He suggested that the translator ought to allow his or her own language to be powerfully affected by the language of the original text. Both Schleiermacher and Benjamin, from somewhat different theological perspectives, insisted that there is a metaphysical imperative to create unreadable, unidiomatic, clunky translations, the kind condemned by non-theorists as 'translationese'.

In recent decades, the two most influential voices in US translation studies, both proponents of 'foreignising' translation styles, have been Antoine Berman and Lawrence Venuti. Both build on the work of Benjamin and Schleiermacher. Berman, whose Polish-Jewish-Yugoslav family spent the Second World War in hiding in France, was highly conscious of the ways that dominant cultures can mistreat immigrants. He claims that translators have an ethical obligation to recognise the differences between their source text and the norms of the translator's linguistic culture, rather than forcing these foreign voices to speak in exactly the same way as their hosts.

Berman died in 1991 at the age of only forty-nine, but some of his legacy is perpetuated in the work of Lawrence Venuti, an American translator of Italian novels and a professor at Temple University, who is the best-known name in contemporary translation theory. Venuti has written passionately (most influentially in *The Translator's Invisibility*, 1995) against the prevailing anglophone idea that translations of non-anglophone literature should mask their own status as translations. He argues that translators, and their publishers, need to make themselves more visible to combat the stranglehold of English on the global literary marketplace.

But other practising anglophone translators have insisted that the primary imperatives for a responsible practice of literary translation are not ideological or political, but writerly. Susan Bernofsky has noted that a translator must, above all, 'be a writer', which may entail 'pushing the boundaries of language', in the service of literary art. Damion Searls' lively book, *The Philosophy of Translation* (2024), develops this insight, showing the reader that the translator is not merely a 'copyist', but a creator, who is 'necessarily producing new work in and for a new context'. A translator who fails to think hard enough about how to use the resources of her own language, and the expectations of the translation's readers, will almost certainly produce a stylistically muddled, ineffective text. As Guy Davenport noted in a damning essay on Lattimore's translation of the *Odyssey* (published in the journal *Arion*, spring 1968), 'Translation involves two languages; the translator is in constant danger of inventing a third that lies between, a treacherous non-existent language suggested by the original and not recognized by the language into which the original is being transposed.' It is never enough to ask if a translator knows the source language well enough to translate from it; we must also ask whether she is a good enough writer of English to create something that will live on its own.

By this light, what matters most about *The Vegetarian* is not whether Smith preserved Han's syntax (she certainly did not), but whether she managed to turn an important work of Korean literature into a novel that was equally powerful in English translation. A similar test case is provided by Ezra Pound's famously controversial imitation (not quite 'translation') of Li Po's 'The River Merchant's Wife: A Letter'. Pound played fast and loose with the original Chinese poem, which he could not read, and catered to Western stereotypes about East Asian literary culture. And yet for many anglophone readers the result is a moving English poem in its own right.

Venuti associates fluent, readable, domesticising translation practices with political conservatism in general – a link that may fit some cases, but not others. Schleiermacher was originally interested in 'foreignising' for reasons of German nationalism: by bringing in more foreign voices, translators could extend the 'boundaries of the German language'. Difficult, unreadable translations are not inherently more ethical or ideologically superior to more fluent or domesticising ones, and the creation of a more reader-friendly translation does not necessarily imply a desire to appropriate or 'colonise' the foreign original.

The imperative always to foreignise implies a refusal to consider the needs and desires of non-expert readers, including students as well as general readers, and the specific, highly variable cultural contexts in which a translation appears. Venuti claims that a translator of an Italian novel has no right to translate *tagliatelle* as 'noodles'. But surely the choice of how to translate *tagliatelle* will have different stakes, depending on the needs and expectations of presumed readers. Like so many translation dilemmas, this choice hinges on the specifics of a particular cultural and literary milieu. *Tagliatelle* is not a markedly Italian or markedly foreign word in its original context, so there is no inherent reason why the English translator should make the food sound stranger than it does in the original. But what is 'strange' is not immutable. Nowadays, many readers will know what *tagliatelle* are, whereas in the mid-twentieth century 'noodles' was a perfectly defensible choice for an American readership – although it would presumably have read as Asian, not Italian, for British readers.

As the pasta example shows, the challenges of translation go far beyond the gaps between antiquity and modernity. There are difficult choices to make when translating ordinary, mundane words as well as fancy, experimental or high-brow literature. A famous Menier chocolate advertisement reads: *Évitez les Contrefaçons*. Is it more 'faithful', more 'responsible', to reflect the original phrasing, 'Avoid the substitutes' – although this is not a sentence that any English speaker would ever utter, least of all when trying to sell something? Or would it be better to use the normal English equivalent, 'Accept no substitutes'? In this and numberless other possible instances, there is no single right answer; it depends on the specific goals of the translator, the linguistic and literary contexts of the translation, and the needs and expectations of particular readers.

Translation is usually imagined as an interaction between two creative individuals: the author and the translator. But there are also many intermediaries involved in the process, including the editors who commission translators to do their work, the publishers who pay for it and market it, the media people who decide whether and how it will be covered, the reviewers who assess how it is to be judged, and the readers who buy it, or refuse to buy it – and in the case of 'canonical' literature, the teachers and scholars who decide which translations to assign to their students. Some of the most successful modern translations have been the result of collaborations between scholars and poets (such as Robert Hass, Robert Pinsky, Seamus Heaney and W. S. Merwin), or between teams of translators (like the one that created the King James Bible, or the Russian classics rendered by Larissa Volokhonsky and Richard Pevear). These cases complicate the question of where the creative energy of a translation comes from.

Translations can confirm cultural prejudices – like Pound with Chinese poetry. But they can also challenge them, shifting the reader's perception about what a particular language or text 'should' sound like. The irruption of strangeness into English, in the form of translated literature, can transform the possibilities for anglophone writers who are not translators. The translations of *Aeneid* books

2 and 4 by Henry Howard, Earl of Surrey in the sixteenth century were foundational for the use of unrhyming iambic pentameter in English. Modern and contemporary poets are able to use numerous originally foreign forms – the sonnet, the villanelle, the haiku, the ghazal – largely thanks to the work of translators. One of my own primary goals in creating retranslations of the *Odyssey* and the *Iliad* was to showcase the new and ongoing possibilities of using traditional, metrical, formal verse. Prose poems and free verse can be wonderful, but they are not the only way to write poetry, even in the twenty-first century.

All literary translators wrestle with the gaps in how two languages individuate the world. In the *Cratylus*, Plato's Socrates suggests that the best, most truthful language will 'carve nature at its joints', as if the world exists already pre-divided into categories, which the user of human language must discern and follow, like a skilful butcher slicing a carcass. Contemporary philosophers debate whether some entities – like, perhaps, chemical elements, or the laws of nature – might be natural kinds. But in the messy, wild world of human language as it is used, words always come trailing a glorious cloud of connotations. This is true even of the ostensibly easiest categories of language, like concrete nouns. An 'oak' in English may be just a tree, but it is also, inevitably, an emblem of England and Englishness itself, while a Latin *quercus* is sacred to Jupiter, and associated with prophecy, the army, and the enduring strength of the Roman people. Ethical and social values are notoriously difficult to translate. To take one of many possible examples, the Roman value of *pietas* (duty/piety/pity/loyalty/self-restraint) has no single exactly corresponding concept in most other languages. But the different syntactical structures of different languages raise even more challenging problems. For instance, a speaker or writer of ancient Greek can use the dual form of verbs or nouns, to signal two, not one or many – but many languages do not have a dual form. In Latin and ancient Greek, the object can precede the verb, and important stylistic effects can be generated from the flexible word order of a highly inflected language. Most of these effects, however, are all but impossible to replicate in English, a language in which syntactical structure is heavily dependent on word order. The idioms, connotations, syntax and assumptions of language are always intertwined with a specific set of social contexts, none of which can be replicated in translation.

But retranslators must also consider a further set of complications, in that readers often come to a translated text with strong assumptions and prejudices about the way it 'should' sound in English, or about the culture from which it originates. Readers of ancient texts in translation are likely to approach them with a very particular set of views. These may include a presupposition that these canonical works will be worthy but dull, probably composed in awkward, archaic, barely readable English, even if the originals are gripping, elegant works of literature. Readers may also have an expectation that ancient literature will always be 'grand' or 'great', and that this grandeur will be expressed in stylistically familiar, thunderously grandiloquent ways, so any flexibility or variety of tone may come as a surprise.

And surprise is precisely the point: it is a waste of time to retranslate a text that already exists in English translation unless the translator can offer a truthfully fresh portrait, shedding new light on a supposedly familiar original.

Translation has the almost magical power to bring foreign viewpoints into monoglot minds and lives. As Susan Sontag argued (in 'The World as India', 2007) translation has the ethical task of reminding us that 'other people, people different from us, really do exist'. This is as important for retranslators of ancient literature as for those who work in the contemporary world: translation can reorient readers' sense of the strange and the familiar, and create new awareness of human possibilities. Even in antiquity, people were people, and reading ancient literature should remind us of this essential fact. To perform her challenging task, the translator must think hard about the needs and expectations of her anglophone readers and about the specific capacities of the English language, rather than imposing foreign 'otherness' in a way that is unusable and inaccessible. Unreadable, unidiomatic translations are unlikely to help non-anglophone authors find a wider readership in a world where only 2 or 3 per cent of books published in the US and UK are literary translations. From the deep and intimate interaction between original text and translator, if all goes well, something strange and surprising can come into being – even from the ostensibly familiar world of the ancient past. The shock of the foreign can ignite new sparks in the receiving culture, even when the translated text is canonical and ostensibly familiar – as Cicero and his Roman contemporaries well knew.

WEB OF ROME: HOW THE ROMANS ADOPTED GREEK CULTURE

In a famous short story by G. K. Chesterton, 'The Invisible Man', the murderer enters the house of the victim observed by several witnesses. But they all claim that they saw 'nobody', because the killer was dressed as a postman. The situation of watching a person in the correct uniform delivering the mail was too common to register as an event. Chesterton's hero, Father Brown, specialises in noticing the commonplace things that nobody else can see because they have become too familiar. In the mode of Father Brown, we should learn to notice and be amazed by the obvious facts about Roman literature that are all too easy to take for granted. There are three interrelated well-known facts. The first is that the Romans wrote literature at all – something that was by no means inevitable, since many thriving cultures, ancient and modern, have not done so. The second is that they learned Greek, the language of a people they had conquered. The third, which does not follow from the second, is that they also translated Greek literature into Latin, and imitated Greek literary models – an action unparalleled in the ancient world.

To begin with literature: it is quite possible for a highly sophisticated culture to produce nothing that we in the modern world would recognise as 'literature'. The Etruscans produced great works of sculpture, and had a complex set of religious practices and a sophisticated theatrical tradition; but they seem to have produced little in the way of written texts except a few manuals on divination – despite a deep awareness of Greek culture and its mythology. Scholars regularly bemoan the supposed loss of Carthaginian literature during the sack of the city by the Romans, since it seems natural to assume that a great empire must have produced epic poems and histories on the Graeco-Roman model. But what if there was never any Carthaginian literature? The Carthaginian language, Punic, was never the vehicle for any significant literary culture. It was used to write agricultural treatises and not a lot else, at least according to the evidence we have. There are references to 'Punic books', but this need not mean 'literature in Punic'; it may well mean only that there were numerous books in Greek owned by Carthaginian libraries or book collectors. Ancient Egyptian poetry and narrative texts exist, of course, as do texts in Sumerian and Babylonian; but these were scribal cultures, in which only a tiny minority of the population, trained specialists, were literate. The handful of poems and stories we have from ancient Egypt are not written for a 'general reading public', since no such public existed.

At the very least, no other ancient Mediterranean culture that we know of had anything like the scale and diversity of Greek literature, and no other ancient Mediterranean culture created a wholesale imitation of the Greek literary tradition in its own vernacular, as the Romans did. Of course, the distinctiveness of Roman literary history does not imply that the Romans were superior to other ancient peoples. But the Roman cultural experiment does raise a puzzle worth addressing. Why did it happen?

The answer begins with the Greeks, who were the creators of most of the literary genres taken over by the Romans. The development of Greek literature and mythology was closely aligned to the specific challenges of Greek geography and economic history. The Greek-speaking Myceneans had used writing (a system called Linear B) primarily for palace record-keeping. After the collapse of Mycenean civilisation (around 1200–1050 BCE), Greek speakers lost literacy, or rather people no longer had a use for it, since it had been a tool used by rich, powerful men to maintain and track their accumulated wealth in one place. During the illiterate, more scattered, less urban and more egalitarian Iron Age, Greek speakers, now equipped with strong iron tools and weapons, grew in number and spread out over a much wider territory, forming new cities and colonies in many more areas of the Mediterranean world, including what is now southern Italy and Sicily, Asia Minor, Cyprus, Libya and the Black Sea. In this time of massive social and economic change, Greek speakers developed poetic, musical forms of oral storytelling, including tales of a previous great age of heroes, who were closer to gods than people in the present, and a pair of great wars, in Troy and in Thebes.

In the eighth century BCE (the mid-700s), the Greek

world again became literate, using an adapted form of the Phoenician system. Sometime fairly soon after this, writing was used for a new purpose: to create and preserve works of poetry, based on the existing oral genres of heroic song, hymns, laments and mockery. The poems of Homer and Hesiod came into being with the use of writing – although we still do not know exactly how it happened. Once these great works existed as texts, they could then be learned by heart and recited by *rhapsodes* (poetry-performers) all over the Greek-speaking world, creating a set of relatively coherent shared cultural touchstones. The creation of literary texts allowed people who spoke very different dialects, dispersed across vast distances, to identify with a common heritage, laying claim to a Panhellenic identity.

Then, in the fifth century BCE, the scattered, disparate set of Greek-speaking settlements faced a new challenge: the Persian Achaemenid Empire to their east. The Persians controlled many Greek cities in Asia Minor, but when some of those regions rebelled against imperial control the empire fought back, launching a series of invasions into independent Greek territory. In two much-celebrated battles – Marathon, in 490 BCE, and Salamis and Platea in 480 and 479 BCE respectively – the Athenians managed to resist Persian invasion and maintain their independence.

All this matters for literary history, because the Athenians – who had recently cast off a set of domestic tyrants and instituted a set of democratic reforms to make their city-state at least somewhat more egalitarian – prided themselves on cleverness, speech, art and culture, as well as military might. Over the course of the fifth century, intellectuals and orators flocked to Athens from all over the Greek-speaking world, sharing ideas and generating new genres of discourse, including historiography, medical writing and ethnography. The city's civic and religious festivals centred performances of poetry, including the traditional works of Homer and Hesiod, and also new kinds of musical poetic performance, such as comedy, satyr plays, dithyramb, and the city's most popular poetic product: tragedy. Athens's period of economic and military success was relatively short-lived: the city fought a long and expensive war with their neighbours, the Spartans, for the last third of the fifth century, and lost definitively in 404 BCE. But even in the succeeding centuries – during the dominance of the Macedonian Empire, then the Hellenistic Kingdoms (after Alexander the Great), and even after the rise of Rome – Greek poets and prose writers constantly looked back to the archaic poetry of Homer and Hesiod, and classical Athenian works by poets like Sophocles and writers like Thucydides and Lysias. The strong and coherent tradition of Greek literary production created a sense of cultural identity even as the social and economic position of Greek speakers changed wildly.

Similarly, the creation of Roman literature, based directly on the Greek tradition, allowed the diverse citizens of what was eventually a vast empire to maintain a sense of connected identity. It all began, we are told, in 240 BCE, when Livius Andronicus created a Latin play translated from an Athenian drama, which was performed at the official Roman Games (*Ludi Romani*) to celebrate Roman military victories. This was, as far as we know, the first time that a translation of any Athenian dramatic script had been staged. Many other ancient cultures were heavily influenced by the Greeks and were aware of their literature, including the Romans themselves for many generations. But nobody until Livius Andronicus had translated it. The *Ludi Romani* had been held for generations, and nobody before 240 BCE seems to have felt that the occasion demanded Latin drama in the Athenian mould.

Hellenisation was, in itself, nothing new in the Roman culture of the third century BCE. The earliest known Latin hymns already show signs of Greek influence, and there is no evidence of entirely pre-Greek Latin literary culture. But the piecemeal adoption of Greek formulae, myths and tropes in short songs is quite different from what began to happen in 240: the translation of whole Greek texts, and soon, the writing of Latin epic and drama based on Greek forms, Greek metres and Greek mythology. Why did the Romans suddenly switch in 240 from their tradition of half-heartedly borrowing various bits from Hellenic literary culture to this monstrous adoption of the whole hog?

The answer must have to do with Rome's extraordinarily rapid and very recent military success. The Romans had defeated Carthage in the First (or 'Great') Punic War just a year before these crucial Roman Games. The war ended in 241 BCE with the Carthaginians signing a peace treaty, in which they agreed to cede Sicily to the Romans, who then, for the first time, had control over the whole of the Italian peninsula. In his book *Beyond Greek* (2016), Denis Feeney argues that the Romans used the Games as part of a 'new international dialogue', asserting their power and cultural credibility to the rest of the Mediterranean world.

The paradox that Rome, the military conqueror of Greece (both the territory known as 'Big Greece', Magna Graecia, in 241 BCE, and Greece proper in the Battle of Corinth, 146 BCE), was 'conquered' by Greek literature and culture, has been well known since the time of the Roman poet Horace. But one may still marvel at it, and wonder, in particular, how the Romans managed so quickly to absorb the whole tradition of Greek literature, and use it as the basis of a thriving literary tradition of their own.

Most ancient elite cultures were monolingual, just as modern anglophone elites are. According to recent Pew Research Center data, over 33 million Hispanics in the United States speak English 'proficiently', making up about 68 per cent of all American Hispanics over the age of five; less than 2 per cent speak no English at all. By contrast, according to a Gallup poll from a few years ago, only 22 per cent of non-Hispanic Americans are at all proficient in any language other than English; less than 10 per cent can hold a conversation in Spanish. Most non-Hispanic North Americans have no shame about their linguistic and cultural ignorance, while many believe that all citizens 'should speak English' – a rallying cry of several Republican campaigns. The dominance of English is equally visible in cases where non-anglophone popular fiction (like the novels of Henning Mankell or Stieg Larsson) is imported to anglophone cultures, with its foreignness carefully managed and partially erased. All this is just as we would expect. Members of a dominant culture impose their own linguistic norms on social groups that have less political and economic power. It would have been very surprising if the colonists of Jamestown, Virginia, in the seventeenth century, had made a serious effort to learn the Algonquian languages, just as it would if the anglophone inhabitants of contemporary London felt the need to learn Romanian.

In the ancient world full bilingualism was not the norm, even when two cultures lived very closely with one another – as they did, for example, in Alexandria under Macedonian Greek rule. The ruling family, the Ptolemies, did not bother to learn Egyptian until the end of the dynasty – Cleopatra VII may have been the first to learn the language – while the Egyptians learned Greek. Alexandria is, then, in some ways a parallel case to the modern United States: the dominant culture imposed its linguistic norms on the people it ruled. But the relationship is a little more complex than this may suggest. The Egyptians learned Greek but showed no interest in Greek culture (and certainly were never tempted to translate Greek drama into Egyptian), whereas the Greeks were fascinated by Egyptian culture – at least as mediated and fictionalised in Greek sources, such as the obviously outdated, presumably inaccurate, and ever-popular analysis of Egypt by Herodotus. And yet the Greeks felt no urge to learn Egyptian.

By contrast, the Romans learned Greek, and already in the third century BCE, bilingual education was the norm for the elite. One primary reason is that they wanted and needed to prove to their neighbours and new colonial subjects that they were a cultured, sophisticated people with a global outlook – qualities that went without saying for Greeks or Egyptians. Roman willingness to learn Greek was part of a drive to assert themselves on a world stage. Still, one might wonder why the Romans learned Greek, but not Carthaginian or Etruscan or Egyptian (at least not to anything like the same degree). Part of the answer must come from the high prestige of archaic and classical Greek literature and culture across the Mediterranean in the third century BCE. Moreover, Greek literature and Greek mythology were spheres into which the Romans could insert and thus redefine themselves, in ways that would not have been possible with these other neighbouring and conquered cultures. The legend of the Trojan War gave the Romans a way of thinking through their place in space and in history. It allowed them to consider themselves both military conquerors, who might grapple not only with foreigners but with one another (like the Greeks in the *Iliad*), and also admirable non-Greek aliens, like the Trojans from whom the Romans supposedly descended. More broadly, the fact that the Roman elite were not only literate but bilingual gave them a double advantage over the Greekless, and hence 'uneducated', population of the empire that they were rapidly building.

The choice to translate and imitate Greek drama, Greek epic and Greek historiography – rather than make up new forms from scratch (easier said than done) or to develop native Italian forms of song or story – might seem like an admission of weakness. But it was not necessarily so, as Feeney argues in *Beyond Greek*. For one thing, the turn to Greece was a way of rejecting or downplaying links between Rome and its neighbours on the Italian peninsula: the Romans, by swimming with the bigger fish of Greece, could make the Umbrians and Oscans and Etruscans seem invisible. Furthermore, the choice to turn to the prestigious canon of ancient Athenian literature – ignoring all contemporary Greek literature – bolstered the prestige of the Romans in terms that were legible beyond the peninsula. The literature and culture of ancient Greece did not signal 'antiquity', but rather 'power' and 'global reach'. Sicily, newly under Roman sway, was part of Magna Graecia and was full of Greek settlers. Through translating and imitating Greek literary culture, the Romans now demonstrated that they were just as sophisticated as the people they ruled.

The particular uses of Greek culture by the Roman elite, as a means to bolster their prestige in Italy and around the Mediterranean world, may help to explain the unusual facts noted above: that the Romans translated anything at all, and that what they translated was Greek literature rather than non-literary Greek texts. The Romans turned to Athenian tragedy, Greek 'new' comedy, and Homeric epic, but largely ignored Greek scientific and mathematical texts. By contrast, 'literature' in the ancient Mediterranean world was usually not translated: Babylonian and Sumerian epic died with cuneiform, because nobody in antiquity translated *Gilgamesh* into Greek or Latin or Persian – although the myths lived on, recycled into other cultures. The more usual pattern was for technical manuals to be translated into other languages for their practical uses, as the Romans translated Etruscan treatises on divination. Literary translation itself, as opposed to oral interpretation, is not something that exists in every culture, including those with multiple language groups (such as modern India). The Romans translated the Greeks because these two cultures stood in a relationship that was unlike any other in the ancient or perhaps modern worlds, and because Greek culture was uniquely valuable to the Romans in the third century BCE, as they tried to build up a global cultural identity to match their newly acquired empire.

Roman elite men hired Greek men, often enslaved but highly educated immigrants, to tutor their sons. These Greek immigrants were the first 'Roman' authors, and the inventors of Roman literature. Livius Andronicus himself may have been originally a slave, and was certainly a tutor in an elite Roman family. It used to be commonly argued that he produced his translation of the *Odyssey* as a crib, to help his charges trudge through the original. Feeney suggests that Livius may well have been inspired by the common school exercises, which included having the boys translate in two different modes: word for word, and in a looser style, looking for a rhetorical equivalent. Livius Andronicus's own mode of translation in the *Odyssey*, as far as we can tell from the frustratingly limited fragments we have, suggests a lively domesticising style, using a native Italian metre (Saturnians), rather than adapting the Greek hexameter for Latin, and converting the Greek 'Muse' into the native equivalent (*Camena*). Livius himself was not a Roman insider, 'Hellenising' Roman traditions. As a Greek living in Rome, he was immersed in both traditions, and, if anything, he should be seen as Romanising his own native literary heritage, rather than writing as a Roman. All the early Roman writer/translators had complex national and ethnic identities: Naevius spoke Oscan, Greek and Latin; and Ennius, the first great epic poet in Latin, claimed to have 'three hearts' for his three languages (Oscan, Latin and Greek), but he was probably also a native speaker of Messapic. The choice to convert Greek literary forms into Latin was a way for these cosmopolitan intellectuals to straddle two of their own linguistic identities, and to find a place for themselves within the dominant culture. It is no coincidence that classical Latin literature, unlike Greek literature from the pre-Roman periods, is almost entirely composed in the standardised language of the Roman metropolitan elite, rather than a mash-up of local dialects. This global language, and this literature, was manufactured by people from outside the system. Within a generation or two, 'Romans from Rome' were able to create Latin literature, and Latin authors could look back to older Latin predecessors as well as the Greeks – a complex double heritage that gives the Roman tradition much of its distinctive flavour.

It is easy to take history for granted – to assume that what happened must have happened. So it is salutary to remember how easily it could have been otherwise. This applies to iconic moments in military history: the Athenians might have lost at Marathon, and the next few centuries would have been entirely different. The same is true of literary history. The Greeks need not have used writing to transform their poetic traditions into 'literature'. The Romans need not have translated the Greeks, and need not have created their own literary tradition modelled on that earlier one. From our perspective, literary history has always been there, since long before our own time. Remembering the strange constellation of causes and chances that led to its creation may enable us to turn back to the literature of the past with new eyes, ready to be surprised by what we find.

THE TROUBLE WITH SPEECHES: THE BIRTH OF POLITICAL RHETORIC IN AN ANCIENT DEMOCRACY

Greece has had a turbulent economic and political history in the twenty-first century, centring on a major debt crisis in 2009. The recent financial troubles reopened old, even ancient wounds. Greece – located on the eastern fringe of modern Europe – prides itself on being the birthplace not only of many important literary, artistic and scientific traditions (tragedy, comedy, history, philosophy, classical sculpture and architecture, mathematics, medicine, botany and so on), but also of the political structure associated by many with individual liberty. Fifth-century Athens was one of the world's first 'democratic' societies. But the ancient Greeks, like their modern counterparts, experienced constant threats to the freedom that they saw as the primary component of their civilisation.

Ancient Athens was democratic in a very different sense from modern democratic societies, like those of a contemporary European nation, or the United Kingdom, or the United States. In some ways, it involved far more active involvement by the citizens in the process of government:

important decisions, such as whether to go to war or not, or continue a war once begun, were made by the direct vote of all the citizens, not by elected representatives. Citizens actually did show up regularly to vote. This is in contrast to modern democracies: in the United States it is common for half the electorate, usually the poorer half, not to attend the polling stations even for presidential elections, and turnout is even lower in off years and local elections. Most government officials in Athens were appointed from the citizen body by lot, such that everybody whose name was in the lottery had a more or less equal chance of attaining a position of power (again in contrast to many modern societies, in which those with advantaged educational backgrounds and more personal wealth have a far greater chance of attaining public office). On the other hand, the citizen body in ancient Athens was a tiny proportion of the total population: women, enslaved people, and resident aliens ('metics') were excluded, leaving perhaps only about 20 per cent of people living in the city as legal citizens with a right to vote. The *dēmos* – 'people' – had power, *kratos* (hence the system was *dēmokratia*): but the category of 'the people' excluded most living adult human beings within the community. And yet liberty and equality, at least within the small community of male citizens (*isonomia*), were essential elements in the city's self-image. The Athenians were aware of their difference from other Greek city-states, which had either a single ruler (a 'tyrant' – not necessarily a bad word in an ancient context), or an aristocratic ruling party (an oligarchy – rule of the few).

Greek freedom was important in another sense, for the society of Greek speakers as a whole. In the mid-fifth century BCE, it was thanks to the outside threat of the powerful Persians and other 'barbarians' that disparate Greek city-states began to unite together as 'Greece' – at least for a few decades, before the infighting of the thirty-year Peloponnesian War between Athens and Sparta began. The memory of the Persian Wars haunted the later Greek imagination, and helped to form an image of what it meant to be 'Greek', and, later still, shaped what it meant to be 'Western' or 'European', which was contrasted with an image of what it meant to be 'Eastern' or 'Oriental'. Edward Said's influential study of the concept he popularised, 'Orientalism', begins with Greek depictions of the Persian 'other', and argues that the modern European prejudice against the peoples of the Near East was inspired by a reading of the ancient Greek sources. Nineteenth-century historians were glad to find in the ancients apparent confirmation of the view that Easterners tend to be slavish, effeminate and luxury-loving, lacking the backbone and enterprising spirit that are supposedly characteristic of 'Western Man'.

Against the background of all this dreadful ideological baggage and bogus history, we should remember that ancient Greece is a very strange case to use as a symbol of the superior norms of liberty and reason that are supposedly characteristic of Europe or 'the West'. Greece in general, and Athens in particular, has had a messy, chaotic history in which lack of liberty has always been the norm for the majority of inhabitants. In antiquity, 'Greece' was a collection of city-states, in which people spoke many different dialects and were engaged in a constant struggle for dominance – a situation reflected in the first work of Greek literature, the *Iliad*, which is all about the conflict between two Greek chieftains (the Homeric word is *basileus*, sometimes misleadingly rendered 'king'), Achilles and Agamemnon, each of whom is the big cheese in a different patch of territory. Tyrants ruled many Greek city-states, including Athens before the fifth century. Moreover, Athens had political and military dominance in the Greek world for only the brief period – less than fifty years – between Plataea (479 BCE) and the Peloponnesian War (431 BCE). Then oligarchic Sparta and oligarchic Thebes each in turn gained control, until Greece was united only in defeat, overtaken by a series of foreign overlords.

Modern Greece dates back only to 1821, when the Greeks finally threw off Ottoman rule. The poet Byron, who died trying to fight in the Greek war of independence, movingly links this modern war with the ancient battle of Marathon, the earlier moment when Greece achieved freedom from Eastern oppression, ventriloquising the voice of a native Greek bard, a modern Homer (this is from *Don Juan*, a lyric from Canto 3, inserted after stanza 86):

> The mountains look on Marathon –
> And Marathon looks on the sea;
> And musing there an hour alone,
> I dream'd that Greece might still be free.
> For, standing on the Persians' grave,
> I could not deem myself a slave.

But 'slaves', or at least colonial subjects of a larger imperial power, are what Greeks usually were. Before the Ottomans, Greece had been, for a thousand years, under the control of the Byzantine Empire. Before the Byzantines, the Romans ruled Greece, and before them, Macedonia.

The Battle of Chaeronea, in 338 BCE, is in this context the most important turning point in Greek history. That was the moment when Philip of Macedon invaded the Greek province of Boeotia and achieved a decisive victory, wiping out even the Sacred Band of Thebes, a military group that had previously been considered invincible thanks to their mutual loyalty and courage. A famous statue commemorating them, the Lion of Chaeronea, stands in the modern town of Chaeronea, discovered and re-erected by English travellers in 1818, at the time of the modern Greek struggle for independence. The ideal of Greek liberty was influential and inspiring both to the Greeks themselves and to non-Greeks precisely because it flourished so briefly, and ended so soon.

The Battle of Chaeronea is an essential moment in the nostalgic, idealised vision of Greek liberty: it was the ultimate great heroic fight for Greek 'liberty' against a 'barbarian' ruler. These are the terms in which we still remember that historical turning point, because they are the terms used by the loudest and most influential voice in Greek politics at the time: that of Demosthenes, the last and the greatest spokesman for ancient Athenian freedom.

Demosthenes – an Athenian lawyer, speechwriter, ambassador, politician and demagogue – made a pile of money from his skill in the law courts, and then launched a new political career founded on hostility to Philip of Macedon: he constantly urged his fellow citizens to fight off the foreign invader. His childhood and youth, about which we know far more than we do for almost any other ancient historical figure, are fascinating in themselves, and vividly narrated by Plutarch in his wonderful *Life of Demosthenes*.

Our hero's father, also named Demosthenes, was a prosperous small-business owner, who employed more than fifty slaves manufacturing weapons and furniture. The father died when Demosthenes Junior was only seven years old, and left instructions in his will that the estate should be managed by his relatives, one of whom was also supposed to marry the dead man's widow, and another, his daughter. The guardians were to oversee the younger Demosthenes' education and ensure that when he grew up he would receive full control of the workshops, along with the profits. But the guardians betrayed the trust, kept the money for themselves, and ruined the business, leaving the boy almost destitute. According to some versions of the story, they also failed to provide for his education, although this seems implausible, since Demosthenes himself acknowledges that his guardians failed to pay the tutor's fees only temporarily. Demosthenes was, we are told, a sickly child, afflicted with a speech impediment – though this may be the stuff of biographical legend, since it makes such an appealing story to imagine that the greatest orator of all antiquity was once a poor crippled boy with a stutter. If true, it means that by dint of pure will this stuttering boy managed, against all odds, to mould his frail voice into an extraordinarily powerful trumpet.

According to Plutarch, Demosthenes was inspired by hearing a famous orator speaking in the marketplace, and resolved to learn how to do the same himself. He trained with the help of theatre actors as well as tutors of rhetoric, and is said to have cured himself of the stutter by all kinds of wonderful devices: filling his mouth with pebbles before speaking, delivering his speeches while running uphill at top speed, and by speaking directly to the crashing waves of the sea to prepare for the noise of the Assembly. He would shut himself up in a cave or cellar and shave half his head while studying his presentation, to prevent himself from appearing in public before his speech was fully prepared. The hard work and ingenious training methods paid off: Demosthenes was able to take his guardians to court and sue them for his inheritance.

The story would be uplifting enough if it ended there. But in the course of training for a single personal fight, Demosthenes also prepared himself to be a great lawyer – and, in the end, a great advocate for the whole of Greece. He was a successful private speechwriter, first for individual cases such as his own, before taking on a wider range of advocacy work and becoming increasingly influential in politics. He began to make a name for himself politically, arguing that the Greeks should trust their abilities to fight back against Philip. He would later develop the theme in the Olynthiac speeches in 349 BCE (named for the city of Olynthus, an ally of Athens that was threatened by the

Macedonians), in which he worked hard to present Philip as a super-villain – themes that recurred even more vehemently in his later public speeches.

In addition to speech-writing, Demosthenes also served as ambassador on behalf of Athens in various attempts to negotiate peace with Philip. In 339, he spoke vehemently in favour of the idea that the most powerful Greek states of the period, Athens and Thebes, ought to form an alliance and hold out against Philip – a policy that was highly controversial at the time, and which accrued further criticism and recrimination in later years. The strategy failed, and Philip won at Chaeronea – a rout in which a huge number of the Greek soldiers were slaughtered. But Demosthenes, who fought in the battle along with perhaps 6,000 other citizens of Athens, survived.

In the aftermath, Demosthenes encountered biting criticisms from his fellow Athenians. There were the predictable accusations of cowardice at Chaeronea: survivors always get a bad rap. There were also more substantive suggestions that the advice he had given, to hold out for freedom against Philip, led to a worse deal for Athens and other Greeks, most notably the Thebans, than they might have gained by more conciliatory rhetoric. But enough of his fellow Athenians saw things his way that Demosthenes was chosen to deliver the funeral oration for those who died at Chaeronea. In this speech, he warmed to the great theme that he would pick up later in his most famous judicial oration, *On the Crown*: the idea that a struggle for freedom is in itself a kind of victory, regardless of the outcome. This latter speech was ostensibly made in defence of a fellow orator, Ctesiphon, but it was ultimately in defence of Demosthenes' own political career and, more broadly, as a celebration of what he presents as the glorious fight for Athenian independence against the threat of imperial control. In Demosthenes' words, the dead preferred 'to die nobly than to live and see Greece suffer misfortune'.

Perhaps unfortunately for Demosthenes, the Macedonian conquest was not as bad for Athens as he had warned. Democratic government was allowed to continue, so that the people – at least, the male people who were not enslaved – were, in a sense, still free, despite being colonial subjects. But things were very different for other Greek city-states, most notably Thebes. Philip was assassinated in 336 BCE, and his son, Alexander, crushed the rebellious Thebans, slaughtering their male citizens and taking some 30,000 inhabitants prisoner.

It was hard for Athenians of this period to know what to make of their recent history, and hence of their own identity. Should they see the Macedonian conquest as a historical inevitability – and the attempts to resist, recommended by Demosthenes, as merely expensive failures, costly in terms of both wealth and Greek lives? Or should they view themselves as a free people, whose heroism was more important than their actual political status, whose essential battles had always been fought for the high ideal of liberty, and whose literal subjugation under Macedonian imperial rule was merely a historical accident? The highly politicised trial of Ctesiphon in 330 BCE, for his support of

Demosthenes, hinged on precisely these issues. Ctesiphon had proposed that Demosthenes be honoured with a crown, but his arch-enemy, the equally brilliant orator Aeschines, countered that Demosthenes' policies over the past seventeen years had actually done enormous damage to his country. Aeschines took Ctesiphon to court, and contended that the attempt to award a crown to Demosthenes was illegal, since he still held public office at the time, and also because the proposal was made in the theatre rather than the public Assembly (the proper place for the pronunciation of honours).

On all these counts, Aeschines was probably right. It was indeed illegal to award a crown to someone holding public office, and Demosthenes did fit this category. The law against crowning in the theatre seems to have been broken on numerous previous occasions; but here, too, in strict legal terms, Aeschines was correct. Yet the most important issue, and the one that made the trial into a vast political spectacle, attended by onlookers from all over Greece, was whether Demosthenes had been right to urge the Athenians to hold out against Macedon. His own claim in *On the Crown* is that this policy, despite its ultimate failure, was more noble than any mere victory could have been:

> But you were not wrong, no, you were not, Athenians, to take on danger for the sake of the freedom and safety of all – I swear by your forefathers who led the fight at Marathon, by those who stood in the ranks at Plataea, by those who fought aboard ship at Salamis

> and Artemisium, and by the many other brave men who lie in the public tombs, all of whom the city buried, deeming them all equally worthy of the same honour. (*On the Crown* 18.208, translated by Harvey Yunis, Texas University Press 2010).

It is striking that the battles Demosthenes cites – Marathon, Salamis and so on – were victories for Athens. Chaeronea, a terrible defeat for Athens, Thebes and Greek freedom, is put in the same category as the glorious successes of the past. It is like listing the Charge of the Light Brigade as a victory for the British, because the needlessly massacred men died with courage.

Demosthenes argued that his life's work was devoted service to the cause of Greek freedom, or rather, the freedom of all humanity. 'Seeing that man trying to enslave all humankind, I stood up against him, and constantly warned and exhorted you not to give way … I was the one, alone out of all the speakers and statesmen, who did not desert my patriotic post in the time of peril.' (Again, the translator is Yunis, 2010). The rhetoric is truly splendid, and it is therefore unsurprising that Demosthenes won the trial. The speech, often said to be the greatest speech by the greatest orator of antiquity, entirely won over the audience. But it moves a very long way from evidence-based argument. For one thing, Demosthenes wildly exaggerates the power of speech, in a world where military and economic power struggles were far more obvious agents of historical change. But one could argue that the battle of Chaeronea was simply the result of Philip of Macedon's ambitions. If this is true, then Demosthenes can hardly be seen as much of a hero: he talked big, but the outcome would have been the same regardless. It is perhaps unsurprising that Alexander the Great, when he took over from his father, Philip, seems to have taken no notice of Demosthenes. He had bigger fish to fry.

If Demosthenes' honed and honeyed words did have any political power, they did far more harm than good. Demosthenes' less hawkish opponents, including Aeschines and Isocrates, had argued for years that a policy of negotiation with Philip would result in a better outcome for Greece. They each had an agenda of their own, but they also had a point. Demosthenes' enemies argued, perfectly plausibly, that the Athenian and Theban deaths at Chaeronea, and later the slaughter of the people of Thebes by Alexander, could all be blamed on Demosthenes – whose policies obviously did not prevent Macedonian domination, and also caused needless Greek deaths. In *On the Crown*, Demosthenes manages to make it seem as if the choice was between dying for freedom and living enslaved. But the choice, for Greeks throughout this period, was far less simple. Total autonomy for all Greek states was impossible. The real questions were how to avoid being obliterated (by Macedonian or Persian emperors), and how to maintain some rights and freedoms and cultural pride, despite the rapidly changing face of global politics.

In his later years, Demosthenes himself acknowledged that Macedonian supremacy was now unavoidable, that resistance was futile. He made what was seen by his political enemies as a hypocritical volte-face, and urged a policy of conciliation with Alexander, recommending that the Athenians should recognise Alexander as a god. In the Harpalus Affair, he was accused of taking bribes, not for the first time, and was brought to trial in 323 BCE. The trial became yet another retrospective assessment of Demosthenes' career in politics, only this time around it went worse for the orator. One of the prosecutors accused him of having fled the battlefield of Chaeronea out of cowardice, and also, more importantly, of having pursued policies through which 'all Greece has fallen into danger, misfortune and disgrace'. Demosthenes was fined and left the city in disgrace.

He used his time in exile to try to unite other Greek cities against the Macedonians, and eventually was welcomed back to Athens after the death of Alexander. But any renewed hopes of Athenian autonomy from Macedonian rule were dashed yet again when Antipater, one of the generals who took control after Alexander's death, imposed harsh new terms on the Greeks under his rule, and began to hunt down the ringleaders who had spoken against the empire, including Demosthenes. The orator fled, but he was captured on the island of Poros in a temple. He said that he wanted to write a last letter to his family, but as he picked up his pen he bit into the end of it – as if thinking what to say – and swallowed the poison that he had kept inside the reed. He died, as he had lived, by the pen.

In his 2012 biography of Demosthenes, Ian Worthington

reflects a common popular framing for this story in suggesting that we can see him as a hero for our own times: an ordinary civilian, 'standing firmly, defiantly, and bravely against tyrannies and totalitarian regimes'. Worthington also works hard to argue that Demosthenes was mostly innocent of the worst charges made against him, including bribery and corruption, flip-flopping and hypocrisy, and rejects the view that Demosthenes masked his own self-serving ambitions with rhetorical claims to care about freedom and the public good. In this mythic reconstruction, Demosthenes may have begun his career motivated largely by the desire for revenge, compounded by self-interest, avarice and ambition, but he became, in his long-standing resistance to Philip, the voice of the people.

But none of this is a convincing argument regarding Demosthenes' true 'intentions' (Worthington's word). We are told twice, in as many pages, that 'Demosthenes the democrat shines through the rhetoric' of the proposals for postmortem honours put forward by the orator's nephew. In fact, rhetoric is not a dark mirror through which the historian, armed with a nice soft cloth and cleaning fluid, discerns the truth. The positions, posturing, lies and half-truths of Athenian oratory in this period are themselves at the centre of the historical story. The success of Demosthenes is a marker of how very difficult it was for Greeks to imagine themselves as colonial subjects.

Demosthenes' motivations were presumably mixed, as human motives tend to be. It is perfectly possible that he believed some of his own claims, and thought of himself as the saviour of Greece. It is also possible that he did not believe a word of it, but that he simply had a sharp eye for the main chance. We cannot gain any access to his inner psychology from the sources we have – speeches composed for law courts and the public Assembly. What we can know, from reading his texts, is how brilliantly he manipulates rhetorical and theatrical tropes.

The more important question is not about Demosthenes' intentions but about the effect of his words. On this question, more critical scholarly studies of his life and work are more persuasive (such as Raphael Sealey's *Demosthenes and His Time: A Study in Defeat*, 1993). The Greeks tried to hold out against imperial domination; when they failed, they liked to kid themselves that their defeat was more noble than any victory could possibly have been. The relevance of the story of Demosthenes for our own times is a reminder that perceived freedom can be a construction of the mind, of speech and of our imaginations – and that these fantasies themselves have military and economic consequences. In 2009, pundits blamed Greece's economic troubles partly on 'delusions of grandeur and a fatal sense of entitlement', which made the country vulnerable to threats to its economic stability and its freedom. One can make similar points about Brexit in the United Kingdom, where voters – misled by rhetoric, anger and a false image of the glory days of Britain – made the economically disastrous decision to leave the European Union. The modern histories of Hungary, Russia and now the United States in the twenty-first century tell similar stories. American voters chose, twice, to elect a president who has been bankrupted, morally and literally, many times over – falling for the enticing lie that he and he alone could restore lost national greatness. People often prefer words, images and big emotions over sober economic truth, even when the ostensibly frail joys of rhetoric result in the loss of substantial benefits, like wealth and freedom. Pride, loss, self-deceit, cowardice and failure: those are terms that Demosthenes' great enemy Aeschines – who went into voluntary exile after his defeat in the 'Crown' trial, and who lived a quiet life teaching rhetoric on Rhodes – would have understood very well.

SLUT-SHAMING HELEN OF TROY

Émile Zola's gripping novel *Nana* (1880) evokes the rise, fall and early death of a sexy blonde teenager, a celebrity actress and prostitute, who takes all of Paris by storm. She destroys every man who crosses her path before herself dying a dismal death of smallpox, portending the fall of the Second Empire. The novel is part of Zola's series on urban industrialisation and its threat to traditional family life. Nana, although theoretically human, is a destructive and powerful machine, the engine of the new civilisation as well as the motor of Zola's melodramatic plot. Her sexual allure, figured as an irresistible scent, is finally transformed into, or revealed as, the seeping putrefaction of the charnel house.

This is one of the most powerful modern versions of a far more widespread misogynistic trope. Heterosexual male desire for a woman who is perceived to be exceptionally attractive is projected onto the woman herself, who is then presented as particularly lustful. Since desire can be experienced as mysterious, bewildering and overwhelming, the woman concerned must be destructive and deceptive, perhaps possessed of magical and mysterious witch-like powers.

In ancient Greek mythology, one of the female characters

who fits this general model is Pandora, the woman sent by Zeus to punish humans for Prometheus's theft of fire and to end the Golden Age, when she opens the jar of death, pain and other evils upon the world. This is a relatively straightforward presentation of the beautiful woman as a mechanism for disaster – a mere instrument of divine vengeance. But Hesiod adds that Pandora herself had agency, 'strength', a 'mind' and a 'voice', allowing her to 'devise' evils for humanity, when she made the fateful choice to open the jar – an action that has obvious sexual overtones. The problem with Pandora, as with all beautiful women in a patriarchal society, is that she is not merely an object, a statue or a jar. The urge to objectify a desirable woman is undermined by the acknowledgement that she might be human; at the same time, her capacity for agency and choice only reinforces her desirability (and makes her seem all the more dangerous).

Ruby Blondell's insightful study of ancient Greek representations of Helen (2013), notes the close connections between her subject and the Pandora myth. Both characters, they argue, are formed in response to cultural anxieties about female beauty and female sexuality, centred on the figure of the *parthenos* – the girl at marriageable age, a liminal figure who must cross from the world of childhood in her father's house to the house of her husband. 'She must be sufficiently reluctant to suggest that she will not stray once she is married, but she must also actively desire her new husband' – a balance that constantly threatens to tip over. Helen, the most famous unfaithful wife in the Western tradition, is figured as a woman who is constantly in this liminal state, and who repeatedly crosses over from one household to another: 'many-manned Helen', as Aeschylus calls her. She was and is the locus for exploring the questions of whether beautiful women are always necessarily bad, and whether female sexual desire is always a force of destruction. She is also – unlike modern versions of the promiscuous or adulterous woman – always presented as at least semi-divine, the ever-young, ever-beautiful daughter of Zeus, worshipped at cult centres all over Greece, especially in her native Sparta. Modern versions of misogyny usually do not account for the possibility that 'bad' women might also be goddesses.

A book about Helen of Troy by television presenter Bettany Hughes (2007) claimed to celebrate 'Helen as a real character from history', while acknowledging that her existence is only 'a possibility' – as if the biography of a mythical character from 3,000 years ago could possibly be reconstructed. Blondell has none of this naïveté: they note explicitly that their subject is a set of cultural tropes, not a historical person. Helen was a construction of the Greek male imagination, and the myths and literary treatments of Helen can teach us nothing about the lives even of women in classical Greece, let alone women in Sparta in the Bronze Age: she is 'a concept, not a person'. But these myths can teach us a great deal about the complex attitudes of ancient Greek men, mostly ancient Athenian men, towards women, female beauty and male desire.

The story goes that Zeus wanted to reduce the human

population, so he arranged for the birth of the two characters who would make the Trojan War inevitable: Achilles and Helen, representing 'seductive female beauty and destructive male strength'. They have in common an extraordinary self-awareness and concern for their future reputations in myth and legend. Both were half-human, half-divine, Achilles being the son of the mortal Peleus by the sea-goddess Thetis, and Helen the daughter of Zeus in the form of a swan and of the Spartan queen Leda. Owing to this parentage, she hatched from an egg – the first mark of her unusual, not-quite-human status. Helen is the only female child of Zeus by a mortal woman, an exceptional woman in this as in other respects. Alternative versions of the myth suggest that she was the daughter of Nemesis, or 'Destruction'.

Helen's beauty is not supposed to be subjective. A key premise of the myth is that she is attractive in some absolute and total way that defies description, and hence can be represented only by entirely conventional means. Helen, like any other desirable woman in the Greek literary tradition, has lovely cheeks, neat ankles and pretty accessories. She is equally irresistible to any and every man. As Blondell neatly puts it, 'A beauty that is in the eye of the beholder may launch a ship or two, but only a beauty upon which all beholders agree can bind a generation of heroic males under oath and generate an enterprise as cataclysmic as the Trojan War.'

From a young age, Helen was at high risk of abduction. When she was still a young girl the Athenian hero Theseus swiped her, but she was retrieved by her magical brothers, the twins Castor and Pollux. A little later, suitors from all over Greece began to court her, and fighting almost broke out among them. But Helen's canny adoptive father, Tyndareus, persuaded them to let Helen decide, and to take an oath that they would all fight together to retrieve her, were she ever to be taken from her future husband. Helen selected Menelaus of Mycenae, whose main advantage was his wealth. But sometime afterwards, a Trojan prince named Paris was appointed to judge between three goddesses, Hera, Athena and Aphrodite. He chose Aphrodite, goddess of love, because she promised him Helen as a reward – the only problem being that Helen was married already. The abduction of Helen caused the Trojan War.

Helen might thus be seen as a mere puppet, the victim of the gods and of the men who wanted her. But as Blondell insists, 'her complicity is essential to her story'. Helen is abducted, but she is never simply passive. She agrees to go with Paris, although different versions of the story suggest different degrees of willingness. Both Paris and Helen are victims of lust, but are still committing an action and hence perhaps incurring moral responsibility for the deaths that result. The verbs most commonly used for Helen's journey are all active: she left, she went, she sailed away.

The Greek texts seem constantly to return to the issue of Helen's responsibility for her actions. If she really did choose to leave her husband, can we forgive her? The poet of the *Iliad* makes her a sympathetic figure by suggesting that she can never forgive herself – while also creating ambiguity about the degree to which she chose to come to Troy. We see her regret about the war and her own awkward position in Troy, and her resistance to the shameful bed she shares with Paris, to which she returns only when threatened by Aphrodite with dreadful consequences, if she fails to do as the goddess demands. Helen in the *Iliad* is aware of her own uncomfortable social role, and of the cold reaction she arouses in others: her almost supernatural self-awareness, and her subordination to Aphrodite, makes it impossible to dismiss this daughter of Zeus as simply unfaithful or bad. In the *Odyssey*, Helen is shown back home with her husband, Menelaus, in an uneasy restoration of domestic harmony. Yet there is no clear line between Helen and the other wives of the poem. Penelope, unlike Helen, sticks to one man; but both are good at weaving and telling stories, and both have a dangerous beauty, which attracts too many suitors and raises inevitable doubts about whether the woman can be trusted to be true to her husband or her word.

The characters surrounding Helen are repeatedly presented as parallel to her, in ways that create mythic symmetries and mythic contrasts. Menelaus is made unmasculine by marrying a woman who is so powerfully feminine that she comes close to achieving masculine kinds of authority. Paris is emasculated in a different way: he is too similar to Helen herself, and his beauty is presented as effeminate and worthy of blame. In tragedy – Aeschylus's tragic trilogy, the *Oresteia*, being the richest example – Helen is a mirror image of her sister Clytemnestra. Both are too clever by half, and both are explicitly blamed for the destruction of their men, although Helen remains the root of all evil. The Chorus in the first of these plays, *Agamemnon*, implies (absurdly) that Helen's adultery is far worse than Clytemnestra's slaughter of her warlord husband.

Helen is a subject in both poetry and prose in the ancient Greek literary tradition, from the Homeric poems, through archaic lyric, to Athenian tragedy, Herodotus, and the rhetorical 'Praise of Helen' texts by Gorgias and Isocrates. These repeated returns to the same mythic figure show an ongoing Greek interest in the relationship between beauty and responsibility, but also show how Greek attitudes towards war and community changed, from the more negative depictions of Helen in texts created during the Peloponnesian War, to Isocrates' comically positive account, written after the fall of Athens and defending Helen as the force who brought all of Greece together, united for a common cause. Each of these writers is conscious of the sound of Helen's name, which sounds similar to the Greek word for Greece (*Hellas*), but also to a verb, *helein*, 'to seize' or 'to destroy' – a homonymity exploited particularly by Aeschylus, who sees Helen as the 'ship-destroyer, man-destroyer, city-destroyer': *helenaus, helenadros, heleptolis*. Helen the Spartan was a fraught anti-heroine at the time of the Peloponnesian War, when Athens was fighting with Sparta.

Why did the Trojans fight a whole war over this woman? Why did the Greeks bother to risk their lives and wealth for somebody else's wife? These questions are central to almost every treatment of the myth, and must be faced by all translators of the Homeric poems and Athenian tragedies focused on Troy, and anyone seeking to adapt these myths for new audiences. The notion that a war could ever be fought just for a woman, however beautiful, was a pointed reminder of how utterly foolish the motivations for warfare tend to be. Herodotus, for example, begins his account of how the wars between east and west, Greece and Persia, first began, with a po-faced but edgy retelling of the myths of Io, Medea and Helen as a series of abductions that set in motion the conflict that would lead to the great Persian Wars in his own day.

In the time of the Peloponnesian War (against Athens's great enemy, Sparta), Euripides retold the story of Helen at least twice over, in completely different ways, each pointing to the extraordinary and unjustifiable human suffering caused by war. In *The Trojan Women*, Helen comes on stage as a mistress of rhetoric, able to defend her own position as victim of men and the gods – although her case is rather undermined by the obvious advantages of her own situation compared with that of the other women (grieving for slaughtered loved ones, reduced to slavery, with only exile to look forward to). The Helen story is transformed again in *Helen*, which dramatises the idea (perhaps invented by the sixth-century lyric poet Stesichorus) that Helen never actually went to Troy in the first place. An image (or *eidolon*) of her was moulded by Hera, and she spent the ten years of the war quite chastely in Egypt, waiting for her beloved husband to come and take her home. But the play actually undermines the contrast on which it relies, between the 'fake' Helen and the real one. These two beautiful images turn out to be indistinguishable, such that, as Blondell suggests, this 'fantasy of female perfection turns out to be, in essence, an illusion'.

It is rare for Greek authors to defend Helen's adultery rather than simply denying that it took place. But Gorgias, the brilliant, stylistically mannered rhetorician of the fifth and fourth centuries BCE, does just that in his *Encomium of Helen*, presenting our heroine as the victim of either deceit or her own weak will: by his argument, nobody is ever really responsible for their own actions. The problem with Helen was not that she was an adulterous woman, but simply that she was human. The piece is clearly designed to shock and entertain an audience ready for new ideas about ethics and human action. A somewhat more serious defence of Helen was composed by Isocrates in the fourth century, once Athens was no longer the dominant power in the region. Isocrates used Helen in a call for Greek unification against barbarian forces. Helen was the MacGuffin who mobilised all Greek men into action, praiseworthy as an emblem of Greece itself: Helen is *Hellas*. This approach to the myth finally does strip Helen of all agency, since she is important not as a person, or even as an erotic object, but only as a prompt for homosocial bonding.

There are hardly any stories about the death of Helen. She is usually imagined as free from the constraints of time, always fixed at the age of a newly-wed bride, always beautiful, always ready to be touched again as if for the very first time. It is possible that the myths became attached to a figure who was originally a prehistoric fertility goddess. She is supposed to have had just one child, a daughter named Hermione, who was herself unable to bear children: infecundity is another mark of Helen's resistance to time.

She was worshipped at Sparta in a shrine that featured the egg from which she hatched and also the sandal that she lost during her elopement: Helen is not only the ancient equivalent of the nineteenth-century 'fallen woman', but also that of Cinderella, the irresistibly pretty young girl for whom it is always midnight as she dashes, half-shod, from one prince to the next, a trope that is very much still present in contemporary TV teen dramas and the endless reruns and revivals of shows like *Sex and the City*.

In Roman literature, Helen became both less central and less radically ambiguous than she had been in the Greek sources. The first Roman emperor, Augustus, instituted new laws to encourage marriage and legitimate childbearing, and in this context it is perhaps not surprising that Virgil's *Aeneid*, composed under Augustus, features the Trojan protagonist, Aeneas, threatening to kill Helen, as the wicked adulteress whose actions caused the destruction of his city. One can also connect Virgil's more negative depiction of Helen to a broader Roman suspicion of rhetoric, lies and dishonesty. Greek writers such as Gorgias could playfully celebrate Helen's association with the slippery powers of seduction, but in Augustan Rome, in the wake of the Roman civil wars, manipulation of imagery was serious business.

In the medieval and early modern periods, new myths about the Trojan War overlaid more ancient ones. In particular, the doomed love story of the young Trojan prince, Troilus, with his faithless girlfriend, Cressida – invented by the twelfth-century French poet Benoît de Sainte-Maure – became central in Trojan narratives, including retellings by Chaucer and Shakespeare. Helen plays an unspeaking bit part in Christopher Marlowe's *Doctor Faustus*, but she is a phantom, perhaps not even a real woman. Cressida, not Helen, proved a more interesting image of the faithless woman for these later cultures, perhaps because her story, unlike Helen's, can be told without the whole apparatus of the pagan gods. Cressida is not a daughter of Zeus (she is the child of a human priest), and she does not get led away by Aphrodite. Instead, she shows normal, mortal, quintessentially female inconstancy. The ancient myths of Helen were often misogynistic, but the modern myths of Cressida were arguably much more so.

For much of the twentieth century, different 'transgressive' heroines from ancient Greek myth attracted more attention than Helen: the androcidal Clytemnestra and the pedicidal Medea had much more obvious appeal in a world where more and more women were trying to reduce their dependence on husband and children (ideally without killing them, but not necessarily). But there has been a resurgence of interest in the Helen story, with the books by Blondell and Hughes, several Helen-themed novels and poetry collections, and a performance piece by Anne Carson that links Helen with Marilyn Monroe (*Norma Jeane Baker of Troy*, 2019). Helen may have become culturally urgent in new ways in the twenty-first century, now that we as a culture are grappling with the questions raised by the myth: whether image is everything, whether our short-term desires will destroy us, whether gender roles are a matter of nature or nurture, and whether women, especially beautiful women, really count as people. In this age of the internet and AI, we may also find new echoes of the Helen myth, in its focus on the proliferation of virtual, unreal images that suck people into obsessive desire and conflict, over beauty, or women, superiority, power, or over nothing at all.

PUNISHMENT BY RADISH

When Cardi B and Megan Thee Stallion released 'WAP' in August 2020, 'conservative' commentators such as Tucker Carlson expressed outrage that the song might corrupt 'your granddaughters'; Alyssa Rosenberg in the *Washington Post* celebrated it as an 'ode to female sexual pleasure'. The video featured the two long-lashed goddesses twerking their way through a gilded McMansion in fabulous candy-coloured outfits, like bethonged Disney princesses. The lyrics create a cluster of ambiguities: are the speakers supposed to be sex workers struggling to pay their college tuition and running in fear from 'the cops', or wealthy A-list celebrities? Or are they, as Black women in a white man's world, both? Do they really want anyone but each other? Do they own the house through which they strut? The song mocks its listeners and viewers for yearning for these superior beings in their state of limitless desire. At the same time, its sly laughter invites us to feel, for a couple of minutes, part of their glittering, multicoloured world.

The song's genius lies in its inventiveness: its mastery of rhythm, and its innovative abundance of metaphors for the 'wet-ass pussy' of its title. You come for the nasty, but you stay for the poetry. The two artists celebrate the power of their bodies to express desire and joy, but more fundamentally, they celebrate their gushing waterfalls of linguistic 'flow'. The joke of the title hinges on the fact that language is both literal and metaphorical: one body part is used as a linguistic modifier for another. The most memorable lines contain no words that would be unsuitable for a nursery school sing-along, but provide brilliantly funny images: 'Swipe your nose like a credit card', 'Get a bucket and a mop', or – climactically – 'Macaroni in a pot'. It's wild and down to earth at the same time, and forever changes the way you think about cooking spaghetti.

Ancient Athenian comedy of the fifth century BCE – mostly known to us through the work of Aristophanes – can be usefully compared to a number of different modern genres. Like television sitcoms, it featured typical or stereotypical characters, and showcased their ridiculous lust, avarice, stupidity and ambition. Like modern stand-up comedians or late-night hosts, comic poets included speeches in their plays in which they railed at the audience about the state of society and their personal grievances. Like *Saturday Night Live*, comedy in fifth-century Athens included caricatures of people who might well have been in the audience – such as Socrates, Euripides or the politician Cleon. Like *The Simpsons* or *30 Rock*, the dialogue had a high rate of jokes per minute, and catered to multiple different audience sensibilities, including a taste for lavatory humour. As in Broadway musicals or on the Disney Channel, characters in lavish costumes were liable to burst into song and dance at any moment – although the male characters wore large strap-on phalluses, which would make a startling addition to *Hannah Montana*. Old Comedy anticipated modern sci-fi and television shows like *The Good Place* in its willingness to carry out fantastical thought experiments (talking frogs, a city of birds, a singing chorus of metaphysically inclined clouds, or, weirdest of all, women with real political power), and considered their social and political repercussions. Like pantomime or Punch and Judy, it included formulaic riffs on falling over, violence and cross-dressing.

But the lush comic hip-hop of Megan Thee Stallion and Cardi B is one of the most useful modern analogues, because it illustrates the core element of Old Comedy that is most often obscured in contemporary anglophone translations – the lyrical flow. Aristophanes, like the creators of 'WAP', was a musician, songwriter, choreographer and poet, and his linguistic effects depend, like theirs, on the artful manipulation of rhythm and sound in words and imagery. The poetic affinity between rap and Old Comedy is explored in Spike Lee's film *Chi-Raq*, a hip-hop adaptation of *Lysistrata* set on the South Side of Chicago. But most modern English translations have done little to represent the lyricism and rhythm of Aristophanic poetics. A notable exception is the wonderful version of *Lysistrata* by Sarah Ruden, who uses brilliantly lively, dirty blank verse, with exuberant and inventive lyrics for the choral passages. For most other translations, imagine a prose 'WAP', stripped of rhyme, rhythm and linguistic dazzle, and you get the problem.

Aaron Poochigian's 2022 translation of four plays of Aristophanes into clear, vivid, metrical verse is one of the best examples of what translators can achieve when paying attention to lyrical flow. Poochigian is a poet who cares deeply about technique, and largely pulls off the difficult trick of making Aristophanes in English sound rhythmical but not obscure or stuffy. There is a moment in *Clouds* when the avaricious protagonist, Strepsiades, discovers to his horror that his son has learned from the school of sophistry, presided over by Socrates, that it is acceptable for sons to beat up their fathers, since in the animal kingdom young chickens do not hesitate to attack their parents. In Poochigian's translation, Strepsiades responds with a well-turned iambic heptameter couplet:

> Well, if you want to copy everything that roosters do,
> why not go eat manure and take a nap atop a perch?

While other translators reach for words like 'cock' and 'peck' to spice up their prose, Poochigian, here as elsewhere, stays close to the Greek and is willing to let the humour (such as it is) emerge, rather than make up new gags of his own. He is also notably restrained in his vocabulary. The Greek word for what the roosters eat is *kopros* (from which we get 'coprophilia' and 'coprophagy'). It's a general term that doesn't refer specifically to animal refuse – unlike the decorous agricultural term chosen by Poochigian, whose chickens are too polite to eat shit. The choice between 'shit' and 'manure' (or 'poop', a baby word that occurs with surprising frequency in Poochigian) illustrates one of the primary challenges of translating texts so full of colloquial, coarse, or even sometimes obscene language. What people find shocking enough to be funny, but not so shocking as to be actually repellent, differs between cultures as well as individuals. A profusion of 'shit', rather than 'poop' or 'manure', might have made Poochigian's translations edgier for some readers, but unsaleable to others.

A related difficulty is the difference between the sexual norms of fifth-century Athens and those of modern English-speaking countries. There is a wonderful set piece in *Clouds* in which the personification of old-fashioned 'Right Argument' (a fuddy-duddy obsessed with the army's glory days and the oiled curves of boys' buttocks at the gym) has an *agōn*, or debate, with new-fangled 'Wrong Argument' (a slick smart-talker with some sleazy hot takes on ancient myths), over which of them has done a better job of educating the young men of Athens. Right accuses Wrong of having sex with other citizens' wives (which is, with comic absurdity, described as a worrying new trend), and remarks that he must have received the usual punishment: a radish in the anus. Wrong retorts that there is nothing wrong with being, as such seducers would be, *euryproktos* ('gape-arse'); most citizens, he says, including the audience, are surely the same. The joke hinges on the assumption, which would have needed no explanation, that a man with non-normative sexual preferences, a *kinaidos*, enjoys both illegal sex with citizen wives and being penetrated by other men (a shameful preference in a society where 'normal' men were supposed to want to be the penetrators of either women or boys). Aristophanes makes humour out of social hypocrisy as well as the eternal hilarity of bum jokes. Poochigian, however, repeatedly translates *euryproktos* as 'faggot' – which makes the joke hinge on a very different set of social prejudices.

Aristophanes is not generally an archaising poet. Despite his skill with rhythm, Poochigian's English often sounds dated, even when there is nothing markedly old-fashioned about the Greek. The supposedly modish Wrong Argument, for instance, refers to 'lusty ladies' and describes the mythical hero Peleus as a 'poor wretch'. Lysistrata, the eponymous heroine of Aristophanes' play about a sex strike to stop the Peloponnesian War, expresses sympathy for the unmarried 'maidens' whom nobody will 'wed' – where, in the Greek, she uses very neutral, not markedly old-fashioned terms for girls (*korē*) and marriage (*gēmai*). A city official, in the same play, complains at the 'feminine licentiousness' of 'wanton' women – where, again, there is nothing particularly archaic about the Greek. The olde-timey language sits oddly with other moments where Poochigian reaches, usually effectively, for more current language, including some very contemporary references – such as 'nasty women', 'chokeholds', 'ballot boxes', 'ravioli' and women who wear a 'bra'.

Many recent translations of Aristophanes have a lot more colloquial, 'adult', and obscene language than Poochigian: there is usually more shit and less poop. The Loeb translator, Jeffrey Henderson, is an authority on obscenity in Old Comedy, and his versions include multiple instances of 'pussy' and 'cock'; Poochigian mostly prefers 'dick' and 'twat'. Though the Spartan Messenger in *Lysistrata* – whose dialect he translates into what he calls a 'country twang specific to no region' – complains that the ladies have locked the menfolk 'outta their vaginas', any approximation to linguistic realism is rather spoiled by the noun. Poochigian's Aristophanes is arguably quite a lot stiffer and less obscene than the original. It would be interesting to read an X-rated reissue of these translations with the archaisms removed and every 'twat' changed to a 'cunt'.

But this mild, poetic version of Old Comedy, whose kicks come from half-rhymes and the showcasing of technique rather than the bad words, has its appeal. Poochigian writes in the introduction that he finds a 'necessary lesson' for contemporary society in Aristophanes' use of obscenity to condemn the 'crude' behaviour of 'a person in power' who 'behaves obscenely'. The translations themselves seem to me to show precisely the opposite: that careful, sometimes childish or archaic language can provide an alternative to the tiresome barrage of outrage and outrageousness that has dominated the media landscape in recent years. Maybe comic obscenity does not seem so funny any more, now that a laughably unqualified perpetrator of sexual assault has twice been elected as president of the United States.

Poochigian's Aristophanes translations, with their clarity and their understated language, allow for a full appreciation of the ways that Aristophanes' central themes still resonate. 'I know that Athens always seems to choose / criminals as her heads of state,' the female protagonist of *Women of the*

Assembly says. 'So, in conclusion, gentlemen, let's hand / the rule of Athens over to the women.' The simple good sense of the idea comes through clearly in Poochigian's plain iambics.

Aristophanes' comedies are primarily concerned with the relationship of cultural to political change. Do culture wars matter? Is transformation possible? The clowning around, the shit jokes, the puns and the talking animals of Old Comedy are interwoven with serious political topics, such as the human and economic cost of the Peloponnesian War (in *Lysistrata*), or the corruption of the young by wrong-headed innovations in education (in *Clouds*), or the founding of an ideal society, minus the humans (in *Birds*), or the wild idea of emancipating women to end political corruption (in *Women of the Assembly*). All of Aristophanes' extant plays – including the seven not translated by Poochigian – focus on social change and the possibility, or impossibility, of a radical solution to a cultural dilemma.

In the conflict between old ways and new ways, Aristophanes often seems to express reactionary nostalgia for the old, and fear of the new. The education of the wisdom-teachers or sophists, for example, is made to seem both ridiculous and dangerous in *Clouds*. In Plato's *Apology* the play is said to have contributed to the case against Socrates. It takes on a frightening new resonance in the 2020s, given the numerous official crackdowns in the US on books, educational initiatives, and institutions that are said to be dangerously 'woke', for any number of specious reasons.

Comic satire is often ultimately on the side of the status

quo. *Lysistrata* and *Women of the Assembly* may seem to propose a radical critique of the disenfranchisement of women in Athenian democracy. But both plays – performed by and for men – reinforce the stereotypical view of Athenian men that women are primarily interested in sex and drinking, and *Lysistrata* ends with the men bonding with one another as they ogle the naked female body of Reconciliation personified. *Lysistrata* seems like an anti-war play; at the same time, it whips up anti-Spartan sentiment by mocking the enemy as idiotic rednecks who talk funny. *Birds*, composed in 414 BCE, immediately after the disastrous Sicilian Expedition, is an escape fantasy, like Euripides' tragedy *Iphigenia in Tauris* (produced in the same year); but the play also seems to acknowledge that escape is implausible, and perhaps not even desirable. The two Athenian protagonists escape to the sky to establish a new, supposedly better society there with the birds – but they end up replicating the imperial ambitions of the human city they have left behind. Aristophanes' comedy frequently acknowledges the possibility that social or political change might be bad (maybe it was better in the old days), while also recognising that change might not even be possible. Some of his best jokes turn on the pretence that people nowadays have been corrupted by new ways – when, in fact, as everyone knows, greed, lust and avarice do not require a teacher.

The Athens of Aristophanes' comedies is a place delicately balanced between two poles – either as a society of limitless possibilities, in which any or everything could happen and the world could be transformed through one ordinary person's brilliant idea, or as a place that exemplifies all the ways that human beings are ridiculously limited, both by our horny, shitty, hungry bodies, and by our gullibility, our selfishness and our egotism. But the dark or cynical elements of Aristophanes rub against moments of lyrical surprise that can be beautiful as well as funny. Poochigian conveys the lyricism and moments of high poetry, as well as the shifts of mood and tone. Take, for instance, this lovely passage from the Chorus of *Birds*:

> Happy our feathered race
> that in the winter needs no woollen clothes,
> nor do the summer sun's extended rays
> with roasting swelter torment us.
> At noontime when the crazed cicada heaves
> shrill hymns into the air, I roost
> among the flowers and leaves
> that fill the meadow's breast.
> All winter in a cave
> we revel with the nymphs. In spring we have
> pure myrtle berries in their white
> blossoms, we have the Graces' garden fruit.

The Greek creates lush sonic effects through the lull of repeated long 'o' sounds and sibilants: it riffs on new trends in musical styles, and idealises even as it mocks the notion that life is better if you're a bird. Poochigian's version seems conscious of anglophone literary resonances (such as Shakespeare's Ariel) and is at its best in the moments when a slightly archaised fantasy is asserted with absolute authority: 'We revel with the nymphs.' The handling of rhythm is uneven, and to my ear the half-rhymes ('have/ cave') sound forced. The choice of 'heaves', presumably for the rhyme, has unfortunate connotations, as does the 'breast' of the meadow, which doesn't quite capture the image suggested by the Greek *kolpos*, a word that can connote breast, lap, fold, or any nurturing safe haven, and hints that the landscape and foliage are tucking themselves around the feathered community. But the translation conjures a world full of lushly unexpected life and playfulness – as well as the pomposity of these birds who believe that their traditional lifestyle is superior to all others.

It is difficult to make comedy funny on the page. This is especially true of a comedy that depends on the use of music and auditory effects: *Birds*, for instance, created a drama almost like *Peter and the Wolf* out of the different instruments associated with different birds. Stage directions never provoke a laugh, but actual stage business often does. The gap between the experience of watching a performance and reading a play is all the wider for plays with a great deal of cultural specificity, from a culture very different from our own. But Poochigian's translated dialogue is clear and accessible, and manages to be funny fairly often – no mean feat. The scene in *Lysistrata* in which Myrrhine teases her ithyphallic husband with never-ending delays and postponements is difficult to mess up; Poochigian's clear language allows us to laugh not only at the man's predicament, but also at his pomposity. Poochigian translates the name Kinesias ('Fucker') as 'Harden', and has him bewail his frustration in suitably ridiculous terms:

She has destroyed me! Killed me! Even worse:
she got me all worked up and then just left.
Oh, what I'm going through! Where will I find a
  lover
now that the fairest of them all has screwed me over?

The fluent iambic rhythm and the quick flip between a conversational and a hyperbolic register make it easy to enjoy a laugh at poor old Harden's ridiculous inflation of his own importance. In another scene in *Women*, a young man bangs on the door of the women's house, hoping to have sex with an attractive young woman – only to be seized by a horny old one. Poochigian borrows a trick from Bart Simpson, when the young man asks for 'Master Bates' (the Greek has a double-entendre place name that would have required a footnote if rendered literally), and insists that he is not 'Mr Fuck' – again instead of a place name joke that would presumably have got a ready laugh from the original audience.

The cultural specificity of Old Comedy often makes the genre seem less readily accessible than Athenian tragedy. Tragedy was performed for audience members from all over the Greek-speaking world, who flocked to the springtime Great Dionysia, held when the seas were once more passable for those outside Athens. Comedy, usually showcased at the Lenaea, a winter festival, speaks to an in-crowd of Athenians. Tragedy draws on the quasi-universal stories of myth; comedy, in Athens, focused on a single community in a very particular place and time. For that reason, comedy is often more useful for social history than tragedy is: Aristophanes provides specific information about attitudes towards politicians, policies and current events, of a kind never found in tragedy. At the same time, the language of Old Comedy is often much more difficult than that of tragedy for non-native speakers (i.e. all of us), because it includes so many colloquial idioms, and so many detailed cultural and political references. After the fall of Athens to Sparta in 404 BCE, comedy – which had been deeply associated with Athens in its prime – gradually transformed into a genre with much less cultural specificity, and much wider appeal, so that it could be turned into an export product for non-Athenians. The latest play of Aristophanes included here, *Women of the Assembly* (produced in 391 BCE) shows a shift in this direction: the riffs on contemporary politics, poets and celebrities are gone, and the Chorus is composed of boring old human beings, rather than animals or abstractions. *Women* fuses the central Old Comedy plot, of a radical solution to a social problem, with the usual story arc of later comedy, in which a central male character manages, despite obstacles, to get laid. New Comedy poets such as Menander – our only surviving exemplar – wrote romantic comedies about the heterosexual love lives of mooning young men, a theme that had no place in Aristophanes but would have a long legacy in Roman and later European and British drama, and remains with us in the Hollywood romcom.

Aristophanes is a vital poet to keep us laughing through the terrifying changes and equally terrifying stagnations of our own world. In our era of cruelty, partisanship and outrage, there is something both comforting and inspiring about the comic model of Aristophanes, with his willingness to poke fun at both hypocritical traditionalists and absurd revolutionaries. Aristophanic comedy offers a compelling model for contemporary comedians and other artists, in its willingness to imagine alternatives to the status quo. Perhaps his memorable comic and poetic artfulness can be an antidote to the dangerous sound bites, falsehoods and simplifications of contemporary political discourse. We could use a lot more macaroni in the pot.

AVE, JEEVES!

Many elements of ancient comedy, and ancient humour more generally, are easy to connect with features of contemporary culture. The comic tropes of hypocrisy, greed, disgust, surprise, falling over, excretion and sexual obscenity never get old, although the specifics of what counts as shocking may vary from one culture to another. And yet there are elements of ancient Greek and Roman culture, such as slavery, that we in the twenty-first century are likely to find too horrifying to be funny – but which were, to the ancients, normal features of life, and also rich sources of laughs.

When the Romans won wars, they brought home large numbers of enslaved foreign prisoners, to work the fields, mills and mines of the countryside, and to provide an enormous range of domestic services for wealthy city-dwellers. Enslaved people did the hard labour, but they were also essential for all the things that made a rich Roman's life comfortable. Most of the work we would classify as the 'service industry' or the 'entertainment industry' was done by slaves. Bath attendants, cooks, babysitters, nurses, tutors, secretaries, prostitutes, weavers, dancers, hairdressers and waiters were all usually slaves; so, probably, were actors (in contrast to ancient Athens, where prominent citizens proudly acted and danced in the theatre). It has been estimated that in the decades following the third and final Punic War, when Rome won its decisive victory over Carthage (146 BCE), some 30 or 40 per cent of the population of Italy were slaves.

Many slaves were literate, some of them very highly educated. Cicero's beloved secretary, Tiro, inventor of the first known system of shorthand, is only the most famous example. But we have no first-person narrative by a slave about his or her experiences – no ancient equivalent of Olaudah Equiano, Harriet Jacobs, Frederick Douglass or Phillis Wheatley. The Roman story of slavery is told from the perspective of the masters. Slavery made Roman cultural life possible, but Roman authors usually either ignored it, or made jokes about it, or turned it into grandiose philosophical metaphors about being 'enslaved' to false beliefs.

Roman comedy – the plays of Plautus (*c.*254–184 BCE) and Terence (*c.*185–159 BCE) – as well as two comic novels, the *Satyricon* by Petronius (who lived a short, eventful life under Nero, *c.*27–66 CE) and the *Golden Ass* by the great orator, neo-Platonist philosopher, priest and magistrate Apuleius (*c.*123–180 CE), give us some of our best evidence as to how free Romans felt about the people they enslaved, lived with, needed and used. The *Golden Ass* includes the most sustained narrative from the perspective of the enslaved. It tells the story of Lucius, whose curiosity leads him to steal a magic ointment from a witch, and rub it on himself in the hope of turning into an owl. Instead, he turns into a donkey, that most put-upon and slavish of animals, and endures a series of cruel and brutal humiliations, and various interesting sexual experiences, before finally eating the roses that break the spell and turn him back into a man. The novel includes an inset narrative that mirrors the main story: the tale of Cupid and Psyche, in which the curiosity of Psyche leads to her own painful odyssey of labours and wanderings as the slave girl of the goddess Venus, until at last she is rescued and deified.

But imagining the comic awfulness of being turned into a slave as punishment for an excessive interest in the lives of the lower orders is not quite the same as sympathising with real enslaved people. Moreover, the startling ending of the novel seems to undo whatever satirical impact the narrative might have had, by suggesting that the whole thing is a religious allegory: Lucius is saved from his metaphorically slavish desires by conversion to the cult of the goddess Isis. As Apuleius's novel reminds us, Roman citizens were aware that they had to be careful even in how they imagined being enslaved. Owning slaves would become more emotionally complicated if enslavers allowed themselves to think too much about the humanity of those they abused. In Rome, only foreigners (*barbari* – non-Latin speakers) could be slaves; the slaves were deliberately 'othered' by both language and race. But, unlike the norms of the later transatlantic slave trade, skin colour provided no clue to the difference between slave and owner. Slaves might talk differently from masters, but they looked disturbingly similar.

One neat solution was provided by Aristotle, who claimed that some people are slaves because they have 'slavish' souls. Unfortunately, it is rather difficult to tell who exactly has a 'slavish soul', unless being enslaved is in itself a marker of the 'slavish soul' (which Aristotle denied). In time of war, it can become awkwardly obvious that enslavement could happen to anybody. Plautus's play *The Captives* seems to deal with precisely this issue: a master changes places with his slave, but both turn out to be of noble birth in their own countries. It is a comedy, so of course both characters are eventually set free, and get to marry the girls of their dreams. But Plautus plays with the possibility of imagining that even good people might be permanently enslaved, through no fault of their own.

Slaves were considered part of the *familia* – the household – and were often buried in the same grave as their masters. Yet they were also human chattel, with no legal or civic rights. Comedy is the genre that most clearly articulates anxieties about these paradoxes, and about social hierarchies in general, showing us sons who refuse to obey their fathers, daughters who run off with the wrong men, wives who commit adultery, and slaves who are far cleverer, more patient and more self-disciplined than their lustful, know-it-all, parsimonious masters. These plays suggest a complex combination of guilt, fear, pride, cruelty and envy in the Roman master's view of his slave.

The attitude of the plays towards women is similarly complicated. Women in Plautus come in three main categories: the desirable, money-grubbing sex worker, the beautiful chaste princess (wife material), and the interfering old mother. Hilarious trouble arises because idiotic young men tend to get the first two categories muddled up, as is easily done. Young fools find themselves raping the princesses and trying to marry the hookers, to the rage of their domineering old fathers – until the wily slaves get it all sorted out for them.

In *Jokes and Their Relation to the Unconscious*, Freud compares jokes with dreams. 'Joke-work', like 'dream-work', uses techniques of displacement and condensation to transform and disguise the fears and desires that our conscious minds do not want to recognise. From a Freudian perspective, the prominence of the 'clever slave' in Roman comedy (the *servus callidus*) might be a symptom of slave-owners' fear of their slaves plotting against them, to cheat them out of their money or position of honour in the household. The plays also use the mediating figure of the slave to deal with the fear of sons rebelling against the *paterfamilias*. The slave often sides with the son against the father, and the rebellious slave may sometimes stand in for the even more threatening figure of the rebellious son. The patriarchal system, which allows for little or no autonomy on the part of the lower members of the household (sons, daughters, wives and slaves), is unstable, since any one of these parties may choose to stand up against the master; and it puts a peculiar kind of pressure on the master's own imaginative world.

For 2,000 years, the comedies of Plautus and Terence were seen as an essential element in the classical canon.

Shakespeare's *Comedy of Errors* is based on Plautus's *Menaechmi*; Molière's *Miser* is a version of Plautus's *Aulularia*. Perhaps an even more fundamental influence on later European literature was Terence's dramatic technique of mixing together two or more Greek plays to create a complex or 'double' plot, which had an important impact on the multiple plots of Elizabethan drama and the modern novel.

Roman comedy was not an obscure genre for any literate person between the sixteenth and the nineteenth century: it was part of every schoolboy's education. Plautus's long-assumed suitability as a school text is one reason so much of it is still extant: we have twenty-one of his plays, compared to only eleven by the Athenian comedian Aristophanes. Roman comedy emerged from a particular cultural historical moment, when Rome was fighting and defeating neighbouring empires – Carthage, Macedon, the Seleucids. It is no coincidence that these plays rely heavily on stock characters who reflect Rome's journey of imperial and military expansion: the Braggart Soldier, the Cook (whose wares come from all over the Mediterranean world), the Foreign Prostitute, and the Evil Pimp or Slave-seller, who profits from the misfortune of others. But enjoyment of the genre does not require any specific knowledge of history or politics. Somebody who reads Plautus without knowing anything about Rome's wars with Carthage will not feel they are missing the jokes. It is important from this perspective that all our extant Roman comedies are *comoediae palliatae* – comedies in Greek costume – as opposed to *comoediae togatae*, comedies in which the actors wore the

Roman toga. The works of Plautus and Terence are set in a fantasy-land version of Greece, marked as an 'elsewhere' by the costumes and the Greek names; it is usually said to be Athens, but it could be anywhere. The Mediterranean of Shakespeare's comedies provides a similar backdrop of unspecific exoticism. Moreover, these plays are all more or less U-rated: sex is often discussed in very decorous terms, and there are fewer jokes about farting or shit than in Aristophanes. Roman comedy provides good clean family entertainment.

But in the twentieth century, Terence and Plautus were dropped from the syllabuses of many schools and universities. As an undergraduate at Oxford studying classics in the early 1990s, I was never asked to read any Roman comedy, and my tutors never made any mention of the genre. The Greek Old Comedy of Aristophanes, on the other hand, was a hot topic. It is not hard to see why Roman comedy should have fallen so dramatically from favour over the last hundred years or so. Ancient slavery was not, of course, identical with domestic service in Europe in the eighteenth and nineteenth centuries. But the experience of living with servants made it relatively easy to imagine what it was like for a Roman to cohabit with his slaves, such that people in the nineteenth century could continue to laugh at the *servus callidus*. But P. G. Wodehouse's Jeeves marks the last hurrah of the comic clever servant, who can arrange and prevent love affairs for his foolish young master. In the later decades of the twentieth century, for almost the first time in the Western tradition, most wealthy or middle-class people began to live without any domestic servants. These days, the enslaved and exploited people who provide our clothes, our entertainment, our food and our artifacts usually live outside our homes, often half a world away.

Historical study begins where identification ends. The fall of the genre's fortunes in the popular imagination coincides with a new wave of scholarly interest in Roman comedy in general, and in Plautus in particular. In the early twentieth century, the study of Greek New Comedy was transformed by some of the most exciting discoveries in the history of classical scholarship. A papyrus codex was found in Egypt in 1905 which included large sections from several plays by one of the great lost authors of antiquity, Menander, the foremost writer of Greek New Comedy. The Old Comedy of Aristophanes was full of surrealist utopian fantasies, obscenity, slapstick and direct political satire. The plays of Menander, by contrast, included few political references, and apparently no ad hominem attacks. There are no choruses of animals or clouds, no gallivanting gods, no dirty jokes. In fact, you could say that there are no jokes of any kind. The plots revolve around a small set of stock elements: exposed children (who never die, and always turn out to be from good families); fathers, who try in vain to control their children's love lives; beautiful courtesans whose looks ensnare lively and supposedly likeable young men; 'parasites', the young men's hangers-on; wily slaves; fate, against which we struggle in vain; and supposed virtue, which always triumphs.

If Livius Andronicus 'created' Roman literature by

translating Greek tragedy into Latin, then his *Achilles*, performed in 240 BCE (immediately after Rome's victory in the first Punic War), marked the beginning of Roman theatre. Plautus is the first Roman author whose work survives, and he too, in some sense, produced translations, from Menander and the other Greek comedians. The dependence of Roman literature on Greek models became a cliché. The Roman poet Horace famously declared that *Graecia capta ferum victorem cepit* ('Captured Greece captured her fierce conqueror'). Rome won on the battlefield, but acknowledged the cultural and literary superiority of Athens. The humble nod to the Greek masters is often a kind of backhanded boasting: Roman authors trumpet their own status by acknowledging their dependence on Hellenic models. Moreover, the Greekness of some Roman authors is often mixed with elements that are very obviously Roman. Plautus, for example, throws in plenty of anachronistic references to Roman customs, which destroy any illusion of realism about his Greek settings. The Prologue to the *Menaechmi* includes a characteristic wave to the Roman audience: '"It all takes place in Athens, folks," is what they say, / So that way everything will seem more Greek to you. / But I reveal the real locations when I speak to you' (the translation is Erich Segal's, in the Oxford World's Classics selection of *Four Comedies* by Plautus, which provides a good introduction to the poet).

Plautus's comedy gives a voice to the inanimate and the voiceless. He constantly resorts to motifs of personification and transformation: parts of the body and household objects are treated as if they were alive. In the *Asinaria*, for example, a slave says: 'I do not want one of us slaves, / my mate the door, to get a beating' (the translation is John Henderson's, 2006). Plautine comedy systematically creates a grey area where we might think there could be no middle ground: between people and non-people. The humour may be seen as self-justificatory: if Plautus can imagine that slaves are just like doors, then there's no harm in beating them up. But it may also seem symptomatic of a fear on the part of the slave-owning classes that at least part of their property may be animate after all. If slaves have eyes, hands, organs and dimensions like their masters, then they also have a clear motive for revenge.

It is also worth noting that the slaves in Plautus never actually get beaten, although they talk about it all the time. Plautine comedy has close affinities with the Roman festival of the Saturnalia, when slaves were, for once, allowed to eat with their masters, and seem to have had much greater freedom of speech and action – at least for the duration of the festival. Comedy, too, depicts a magic world, in which the normal hierarchies are temporarily suspended – only to be reinforced, with a vengeance, at the end of the play or holiday time. From this perspective, the 'carnivalesque' licence of slaves in Roman comedy can be seen as reinforcing a normative social hierarchy. The plays about clever slaves escaping punishment remind us that in the real world, the opposite is usually the case: slaves who take the initiative often get beaten, or crucified. On the other hand, the many disguises and role reversals of comedy also suggest that slaves may not be so different from their owners. Physical violence may be upsetting as well as funny, for an audience that could include members who identified with the slave as well as with the master.

Terence, who lived a generation later than Plautus, might be expected to offer a more sympathetic portrayal of the comic slave. His mother was, we are told by the ancient biographers, a slave, and the poet was brought to Rome from Carthage as a child. He was raised in the household of a rich Roman aristocrat called Terentius Lucanus, and then set free. This would explain his name, *Terentius Afer*: Terence the African. He became a comic poet, and produced six plays in the space of six years (166–160 BCE). He then died young – supposedly in a shipwreck, while trying to transport a collection of Menander's plays to Rome. The story of the death is too good to be likely, but the slavery may well have been real; after all, a high proportion of Rome's population were either slaves or freedmen.

But Terence's comedies will disappoint anybody looking for a direct indictment of Roman slavery from inside the mouth of the horse (or the ass). There is far less business about slaves, whipping and rebellion in Terence than in Plautus, and less frolicking, irrelevant donkey-play in general. The anachronisms, the metatheatrical doodling, the songs, the snooty clever slaves and stupid masters are all toned down in Terence, who is much less interested than Plautus in trying to make us laugh.

The result is a new and intense focus on sexual relationships. These plays offer a fascinating and puzzling glimpse into Roman attitudes towards women as both objects and victims of male sexual desire. Instead of the *servus callidus*, the smart-alec slave, we get new attention to a different comic stereotype: the *bona meretrix*, the escort with a heart of gold. The female characters in Terence – including prostitutes and even mothers and mothers-in-law – are almost all nice, admirable, thoughtful, victimised people. The men almost invariably behave abominably: they get drunk, squabble about money and girls, try (and fail) to trick one another, and rape women without thinking twice. But the plays always invite us to see things from a masculine enslaver's point of view, and we are always asked, at the end, to applaud the marriage of yet another rich young rapist to yet another innocent, well-born, fertile girl. The plays are surprisingly brutal in their analysis of the institution of marriage.

Terence's second play, *The Mother-in-Law*, was apparently a flop in the theatre on two separate occasions (165 and 160 BCE), because the audience was more interested in seeing the rival performances of acrobats and gladiators than in sitting through a sharp dissection of Roman sexual mores. The play provides an interesting variant on the usual theme. Pamphilus ('All-Love'), our hero, has already been married for seven months. It was an arranged marriage, and Pamphilus remained besotted with his mistress, Bacchis, for the first few months after the wedding – so much so that he did not even have sex with his bride, and planned to send her back to her family untouched. But as the play opens, Pamphilus has just found that his feelings for his wife have changed. He is no longer attracted to his mistress, and decides he will keep his wife after all. The only problem is that she has been hidden away in the country by her mother. The big secret is that the wife is having a baby, who must, so Pamphilus believes, be another man's child. Such a blot on his honour can hardly be allowed to live. In fact, after various twists and turns, we learn that the child is the son of Pamphilus after all. Drunk on his way to visit Bacchis one night, he raped a girl – who now turns out to have been his own bride-to-be. A happy ending, of a kind: 'All's well that ends well. Just what two / Young gentlemen of Verona might any day do', as Frederick Clayton comments in a brilliant modern epilogue to the play.

As with Shakespeare's bed tricks, it is hard to know how much we are supposed to mind about the rapes in Terence. They are a useful plot device. The victim can remain relatively respectable and sympathetic in the eyes of the audience; the girl may still make a good wife. The victim in *The Mother-in-Law* is never seen on stage – so there is a limit to how much a theatre audience can care about what happened to her. Still, it is hard not to suspect that these plots play with anxiety as well as with self-satisfaction. Pamphilus never lets his father find out the whole story about the rape, and comments: 'I think it's best if this doesn't turn out the way things do in comedies, where everyone finds out about everything.'

The truth is, of course, that this is a comedy, and the audience, at least, does know 'everything'. But perhaps we, too, are better off not knowing, or not thinking too hard about what we know. In the world of Terence, male promiscuity may threaten every marriage, and make every baby liable to be exposed or killed. The play points directly to an obvious double standard: Pamphilus's infidelities, and his flighty emotional attachments – which will presumably continue – are more or less compatible with his role as a husband, whereas his wife, to keep her good name, may only be raped by her own spouse. As in *Romeo and Juliet* – a love story dependent on Romeo's quick abandonment of Rosalind – fidelity to one true love always means the betrayal of another, earlier love: Bacchis is promptly dumped when Pamphilus falls in love with his wife. Marriage may be the enemy of romance, but as members of a stable society we are still asked to clap for it.

A glance back at Roman comedy, and its Greek models, reminds us that humour is always intimately tied up with current social ideas about manners and order. Ancient comic drama, like the modern TV sitcom, kept audiences entertained through a combination of comfortingly familiar stock types and stereotypical situations, fused with enough linguistic and narrative surprise to generate a dash of unexpected fizz. Comedy needs to feel anarchistic enough to make one laugh, but never enough as to spark a real social revolution. It is tempting to see Roman comedy (and its model, the Greek New Comedy of the fourth century BCE) as the ancient equivalent of the modern feel-good romantic comedy. But these are Meg Ryan dramas without Meg Ryan. The female characters have no voice, and sometimes, as in *The Mother-in-Law*, the main romantic love interest is not even a speaking character in the play. A closer analogy might be found in films centred on non-Anglo-American cultures, which analyse the tensions between modern and traditional sexual norms: Ang Lee's *The Wedding Banquet*, Mira Nair's *Monsoon Wedding*, or (perhaps the most Terentian, and most upsetting) Dover Koshashvili's *Late Marriage*, a Georgian-Israeli movie about a man who finally reconciles himself to the abandonment of his beloved mistress and her child, in order to marry the woman his father has chosen. After all, as Pamphilus remarks, 'I do love her. But family must come first. / Falsehood to family, of all sins, is the worst' (the translation is Frederick Clayton's). 'Family' means here enslavement to a pair of savage masters: fathers and babies.

Terence was known in antiquity for the 'purity' of his language, and schoolmasters in the nineteenth century often justified teaching these unedifying tales of sexual infidelity and filial impiety on that basis. A letter to the *Times* in 1847, quoted by Peter Brown in his introduction to his Oxford translation of Terence (2006), complains, 'The cry of injury to morality is mere twaddle, and it would be a lamentable event if an old and useful stimulant to the study of one of the purest Latin authors were destroyed by such maudlin nonsense.' Brown's own version is serviceable English prose, which might well come to life in production. Brown also supplies useful notes, a bibliography, and fine individual introductions to each play. But Clayton's provides a much more lively and readable version in rhyming couplets (it also has a good introduction by Matthew Leigh, but no notes or full bibliography). The *Don Juan*-ish rhymes sometimes call the shots and the language is inevitably not much like modern spoken English. But at least he does not let you forget that Terence was a poet, and a clear-minded, writerly writer. Most impressively of all, sometimes Clayton's Terence actually seems funny, even in our enlightened day and age.

Inevitably, neither of these good translations is all that much like the Latin of Terence, and readers should choose for themselves. Here is a sample, from Terence's last play, *The Brothers*, in which a killjoy, moralistic old man called Demea comes into conflict with his cakes-and-ale brother, Micio, over the sexual antics of one of Demea's sons. But the roles reverse in the final act. Here is Brown's translation of Demea's final monologue, in which he renounces his grumpy old ways:

> No one has ever done his sums so well in the account book of his life that events, time and experience don't always bring him something new, something to learn from. The result is that you don't know what you thought you knew, and experience teaches you to reject what you thought most important for yourself. That's what has happened to me now: that harsh life that I have lived so far I now abandon when I have almost run its course. Why do I do that? Events themselves have taught me that nothing is better for a man than to be obliging and kind.

This is a respectable, plain version, which tells you what the Latin is about. But the wit and poetic elegance of the original are entirely absent. You would never guess, from this rather boring paragraph of prose, that the original is elegant metrical verse, nor that it is replete with neat alliterations (*putares prima in experienda repudies*) and cleverly arranged word order (in the original final line of the passage cited, 'easy-goingness', *facilitiate* and 'kindness', *clementia*, surround the 'man', *homini*, in the line). Clayton does far more to show us that comic poetry is poetry, although he does not quite manage to replicate Terence's artful manipulations of word order – which is all but impossible in a less inflected language like English. Clayton's translation reminds us that we can find in Terence an ancestor for English comic verse, ranging from *Ralph Roister Doister* through Pope to Bernard Shaw and Ogden Nash. Clayton's Demea sounds like a strangely laid-back, Byronic version of Prospero at the end of *The Tempest*:

His life's account-books no man ever drew up
So well but time, chance, change brings something
  new up,
Some lesson. Your known laws become unknown;
Things prized, when put to fresh proof, you disown.
This is my fate. The hard life that I've led
Till now I leave, my span of life nigh sped.
And why? Because I've found, on fact's own showing
The best thing's to be soft and easy-going.

Demea's choice – to see everything as fun and games, and let morality go hang – is one way to read or watch Roman comedy. Humour, both in antiquity and in later societies, often seems to grapple with serious social dilemmas in an ostensibly revolutionary spirit – only to land back in the status quo. Perhaps, in the end, it's all just a laugh.

SPARROWS AND SCRUBBERS

The mooning young man, crazy in love and beset by disapproving elders and other obstacles that block him from the object of his desires, is a familiar character in modern and early modern poetry, from Petrarch's sonnets to Shakespeare's *Romeo and Juliet*. The latter is often described as a comedy gone wrong: the light-hearted soap-opera plot of star-crossed lovers becomes something very different with the introduction of violent death. Shakespeare's dark take on the romcom plot may seem like a wild departure from tradition. But the Latin texts he read in his grammar-school days – including the comedies of Plautus and Terence, and the love poetry of Catullus and Ovid – would have prepared him to see the generic instability of the young lover trope. The besotted Romeo is familiar from Roman comedy, which regularly centres on the sufferings of elite young men in love, blocked from the girl of their dreams by mean old daddies. But Catullus (84–54 BCE), writing a century after Terence, reinvented this dramatic character for non-dramatic poetry. His poems of desire and yearning invite us to imagine what would happen if the comic plot stops part-way through, or takes a sinister turn – what if Juliet rejects Romeo? What if the young man's desires are never fulfilled? And yet the comic origins of the mopey lover motif are still legible in many of Catullus's love poems, and those of his Roman successors. Catullus is too clever, too hard-nosed not to recognise that the agonised, lustful young man whose voice he articulates so clearly might be a sympathetic or pitiable character – but he might also be a bit of a prick. Catullus's astonishingly varied collection of poems combine lyrical precision and pathos with sharp satire, obscenity and a keen eye for social comedy, even when the target of the joke is someone very much like himself.

Catullus was one of the earliest, liveliest and most influential of all Roman poets. Without Catullus, he of *odi et amo* – 'I hate and I love' – we would not have the radically conflicted emotions of the Petrarchan sonnet (Petrarch loved Catullus). Catullus is a vivid example of an ancient poet whose work was extraordinarily influential upon subsequent literary history and still offers new surprises and possibilities for readers and translators in the twenty-first century.

Catullus did not invent his poetic sensibility out of nowhere. He borrowed metres and themes from his Greek predecessors, including Sappho and other archaic lyric poets, and the artful, allusive, learned poets of Hellenistic Alexandria in Egypt (in the third and second centuries BCE). His verbal inventiveness and his combination of colloquialisms with high literary allusions are familiar from Plautus, as is his combination of aggressively clever comic swagger with an intense focus on domestic, romantic and emotional experiences. The earlier Greek tradition of epigrams and drinking songs, with their interest in the twin themes of mortality and pleasure, also provided Catullus with some of his most powerful material. In what is probably Catullus's most frequently imitated piece, poem 5, *Vivamus, mea Lesbia*, the male speaker urges his female addressee to remember the brevity of mortal human lives, and the terrible permanence of death – and therefore to make love with him and live it up for the brief time they have left. Christopher Marlowe beautifully echoes the first line in his *Passionate Shepherd*: 'Come live with me and be my love.' Catullus's short poem is not particularly comic in tone. And yet one can hear strong notes of Roman comedy in the speaker's awareness that fathers and other elders will foil the romantic desires of the young, and in the poem's awareness that romantic and economic value may be misaligned: '[Let us] value at one farthing all the talk of crabbed old men' (*rumoresque senum severiorum / omnes unius aestimemus assis* in the Goold/Cornish translation, 1913). Translators frequently omit the reference to money: for instance, James Laughlin has 'Let us love each other / caring nothing for what jealous old men may say about us.' But as the wonderfully lively and experimental recent version by Isobel Williams reminds us (*Switch*, 2023), Catullus is a poet of power, bondage, money and social class as well as of love and hatred. Her Catullus promises his beloved, 'We'll set the regulators' / hisses at the lowest rate of interest' – a sentiment worthy of twenty-first-century late capitalism, as much as the economically volatile time of the late Roman Republic.

Born in the provincial northern town of Verona sometime around 84 BCE, Catullus died in Rome, possibly of consumption, about thirty years later. Comparison with Keats may feel inevitable, and Catullus's work has some of the cockney poet's lush appreciation for natural and verbal beauty, his sense of yearning and his formal experimentalism. But Catullus's poetry often has a far more aggressive, satirical edge than, say, *Ode to a Nightingale.* If Catullus is sometimes a whiny young Romeo, he is also a volatile Mercutio: prone to lovely flights of poetic fancy, and quick to anger when slighted. His poetic representation of youthful masculinity is defined not only by obsessive, ambivalent lust, often for a woman and sometimes for a man, but also by equally obsessive interest in his friendships and rivalries with other men. He was an inspiration for the Augustan poets of the subsequent generation: Horace, Virgil, Propertius and Ovid all look back to his work. So do many later European and American poets: Catullus's sparrow poems, for instance, have inspired many English imitations and acts of poetic homage, from John Skelton's remarkable poem 'Phyllyp Sparowe' (written around 1500), to Carol Muske-Dukes' collection *Sparrow* (2003).

Catullus came from a wealthy family; unlike Virgil and Horace, he seems to have had no need to cultivate a rich patron to support him while writing poetry. His father was friendly with Julius Caesar, and often invited him to dinner. Catullus wrote several vicious attacks on Caesar, which suggest that his military campaigns in Britain and Gaul are being criminally mismanaged by his chief engineer

Mamurra, and that they are motivated by revolting avarice and greed on the part of Caesar himself, who is a 'voracious / and shameless gut'. Catullus also sneers at Caesar's bisexual promiscuity: 'They're well matched, that pair of shameless buggers, / Bitch-queens both of them, Caesar and Mamurra' (this is Peter Green's 2005 translation, which recreates the metres of the Latin in English).

According to the salacious ancient biographer Suetonius, Caesar complained that a 'permanent blot' had been put on his name by these poems, but 'when Catullus apologized, Caesar invited him to dinner that very day'. This anecdote could be taken as a sign of Catullus's socially privileged position: as the son of Caesar's friend, he was able to be extremely rude about the most powerful man in the world and get away with it. But it can also be taken to prove Caesar's literary taste. He knew a great poem when he read one, even if it included slander against himself.

It is disturbing to remember that the poems of Catullus might well have been lost to us forever. The classical authors whose work was part of the Byzantine school syllabus, such as Virgil and Cicero, were read and copied many times over, from late antiquity to the Middle Ages. But the poems of Catullus were not a school text, for obvious reasons: he is not an improving author. Our knowledge of his work depends on a single manuscript, which was discovered in a monastery in Verona, Catullus's home town, around the year 1300, copied twice, and then lost again. As a result, the text of Catullus is far more difficult to reconstruct accurately than that of more consistently canonical authors.

Even the order of the poems – which the manuscript sorts into three sets ('polymetric' lyrics in a range of different meters, then long poems, and then short elegiac poems) – may or may not reflect the poet's own arrangement.

If Catullus's work had been lost, it would not have been possible to imagine it. He is a poet of dazzling virtuosity and range. As well as his satirical attacks on Caesar and other acquaintances, he also wrote about sex, marriage, friendship, poetry, travel, loss, anxiety, nature, castration, mythology and religion. He did so in many different poetic sub-genres, with self-conscious precision and verve.

Catullus wrote less than Ovid, but his work is extraordinarily varied: it is difficult for any translator or imitator to capture every Catullan mood equally well. Anne Carson's *Nox* (2010), which fuses a sequence of meditations on the life and premature death of her brother with extensive meditations on Catullus and other ancient authors, creates a vivid sense of the Roman poet's ability to evoke the specificities of place and of loss. By contrast, the more straightforward translations of Peter Green are least successful when Catullus is tender and emotional. When the poet mourns for his dead brother in the beautiful poem 101, Green becomes oddly stiff: 'fortune, alas, has bereft me of your person, / my poor brother, so unjustly taken from me.'

The wild stylistic, tonal and formal variety in the works of Catullus have prompted a strikingly large number of experimental versions, on the rich borderlands between translation, imitation, and jazzy riffs on an original. Louis and Celia Zukofsky produced some wonderfully zany and creative homophonic translations – translations that aim to provide a precise echo not only of the sense and style of the originals, but also of their actual sounds. For instance, Catullus's poem 8 – in which the speaker berates himself for his despair at a bad break-up – begins, in the Latin,

> Miser Catulle, desinas ineptire,
> Et quod vides perisse perditum ducas.

Louis Zukofsky's version wittily imitates the sound of the Latin, while also providing a reasonable approximation of the semantic meaning in English:

> Miss her, Catullus? Don't be so inept to rail
> at what you see perish when perished is the case.

This brilliant example of the translator's art helps to remind us how much is missing in poetic translations that focus only on semantic meaning rather than any of the other elements of the poet's art, including the sound of language. It is, of course, very odd English ('inept to rail'?); but it comes as close as linguistically possible to recreating the original's linguistic music. Zukofsky's translation is best appreciated by somebody who has already read the Latin, and can therefore hear the sonic similarities.

Zukofsky's approach contrasts sharply with that of the Loeb Classical Library, although Loeb translations are also designed to be read alongside the original texts. The series, founded in 1911 by one James Loeb and published by Harvard University Press, provides handy, pocket-sized hardback editions of Greek texts (with green covers) and Latin (red) with facing page translations, usually in quite clunky, often archaising prose – even when the original text is artful poetry. Virginia Woolf celebrated the series soon after it began on the grounds that it offered 'the gift of freedom' to 'the ordinary amateur', whose existence was, through the Loeb Library, both acknowledged and 'to a great extent made respectable'. Yet from the start, people disagreed violently about the extent to which amateurish approaches to classical literature could ever, or should ever, be 'made respectable'. When James Loeb first approached publisher George Macmillan with the idea of publishing affordable translations of Greek and Roman classics alongside their original texts, he was summarily rebuffed: 'I am sorry to say that we cannot form a favourable opinion of it from any point of view.'

Indeed, the Loebs for many decades seemed fated to fall between two stools. Their versions of Greek and Latin texts were often not accurate or informative enough about the textual history of the originals to be usable by scholars, plenty of whom considered the series the death knell for true classical scholarship, an endorsement of the schoolboy habit of using 'cribs' to get through Latin class. Meanwhile, those who turned to the right-hand, English page of the old Loebs encountered a text that could be next to impenetrable. Even perfectly decent texts, like the *Odyssey*, were consistently translated into a stilted language that only very rarely resembled contemporary English. Notorious for their bowdlerised translations of the more risqué classical authors, the volumes often lapsed into Latin to handle the dirty bits of Greek authors, or Italian when dealing with the ribald Romans. In the case of Catullus, the original Loeb translation – written in 1904 by Francis Warre Cornish, a teacher at Eton – went so far as to omit whole sections of the poems themselves. For instance, poem 16 begins and ends, *Pedicabo ego vos et irrumabo* – a threat to the poet's rivals that he will fuck them both in the mouth and the anus. Cornish, clearly despairing of being able to make this material suitable reading for his young charges, decorously omits most of the poem, titling it, 'XVI (a fragment)'. The revised Loeb translation, by G. P. Goold (1983), is more committed to the scholarly project of rendering everything Catullus actually wrote, and offers, 'I'll bugger you and stuff you'. This gets both the point and the attitude across – and yet it does nothing to remind us that Catullus, for all his obscenity of language and sentiment, was also composing an elegant, metrical poem, as well as using dirty words. Other translations manage to match not only Catullus's sexualised aggression, but also his humour and love of language: 'I'll snag you and gag you', as Roy Arthur Swanson renders it, or 'Up yours and sucks!' as Peter Green has it – a playground insult with as much comedy as hatred. More literal translations of this poem, such as Guy Lee's 'I'll bugger you and stuff your gobs', often sound too bizarre to be funny.

The enduring image of Catullus is as a tormented young poet, in love with a married lady (Lesbia was supposedly modelled on a real woman, the well-connected and well-educated Clodia Metelli). Yet there is more to Catullus than the intense young man evoked in Yeats' great poem 'The Scholars', whose lines were 'rhymed out in love's despair' only to be misunderstood by dry-as-dust scholars. Catullus was a hate poet as well as a love poet; his work is macho, self-pitying, cruel, technically masterful and supremely funny – even in the Lesbia poems, where he often mocks both himself and his beloved, even while articulating his pain and his desire. For instance, here is one of Catullus's most famous poems (poem 2, *Passer, deliciae meae puellae*), in which the poet envies his girlfriend's pet bird.

> Sparrow, precious darling of my sweetheart,
> always her plaything, held fast in her bosom,
> whom she loves to provoke with outstretched finger,
> tempting the little pecker to nip harder;
> when my incandescent longing fancies
> just a smidgin of fun and games and comfort
> for the pain she's feeling (I believe it!),
> something to lighten that too-heavy ardor –
> how I wish I could sport with you as she does,
> bring some relief to the spirit's black depression!

This translation, by Peter Green, imitates Catullus's characteristic metre, hendecasyllables: his English lines, like those of the Latin original, have eleven syllables each. Green also reflects Catullus's playful combination of linguistic registers, with his combination of 'incandescent' with 'smidgin': in the Latin, diminutives (like *solaciolum*, 'an itsy little bit of comfort', and *aureolus*, 'goldeny') are juxtaposed with simpler and grander word choices.

Catullus's choice of pet for his girlfriend clearly had a literary motive. Sparrows in real life are more or less untameable, but they are the birds that draw Aphrodite's chariot in Sappho's first poem, to bring her to the poet in times of emotional trouble. Lesbia, it seems, is like a Sapphic goddess of love, but one who is not going anywhere. Catullus also draws on a frivolous Hellenistic tradition of hymn-like poems addressed to the most insignificant members of the animal kingdom, such as the locust and the cicada; but he uses this trivial sub-genre to evoke serious emotions – longing, alienation, melancholy. The sparrow seems at first to have usurped the place Catullus wants for himself: the girl holds him in her 'bosom' (the word 'sinus' can also mean 'lap' or 'vagina'). The relationship between girl and bird is vaguely sexual. Green's use of the word 'pecker' is a brilliant hint at the fact that *passer* in Latin, which means 'sparrow', was also a slang word for 'penis'. Catullus was obviously conscious of this double entendre, although it is a simplification to regard it as the key to the whole poem. By the end, it becomes clear that Catullus envies the girl as much as the bird. Although the poem seems at first to be about a comic love triangle – man, woman and bird – it concentrates finally on two incompatible experiences of desire and pain: the girl can find comfort and relief from a plaything, but the speaker cannot. And yet on another level, the poem itself is Catullus's sparrow: poetry is a game, which may or may not offer the poet consolation in times of suffering. A meta-poetic interpretation is suggested by later Roman imitations of Catullus's sparrow poems by Ovid and Martial.

The combination of poetic and linguistic artfulness with emotional and tonal complexity makes Catullus one of the most interesting ancient poets for understanding the challenges of translation and of retranslation, and may also illustrate some of the pitfalls inherent in a 'literal' translation of poetry. One of the best translations of the complete Catullus before Green was the impressively laconic verse rendition produced in 1990 by Guy Lee. Like Green, Lee includes the Latin text facing his English; like Green, he aims for a line-by-line equivalence to the Latin. But the feel of his Catullus is very different. Here, for comparison, is his version of poem 2:

> Sparrow, my girl's darling,
> Whom she plays with, whom she cuddles,
> Whom she likes to tempt with finger-
> Tip and teases to nip harder
> When my own bright-eyed desire
> Fancies some endearing fun
> And a small solace for her pain,
> I suppose, so heavy passion then rests:
> Would I could play with you as she does
> And lighten the spirit's gloomy cares!

Lee's version is in some places further from the Latin

than Green's: 'cuddles' omits the gestural detail conveyed by 'held fast in her bosom', and arguably sounds too infantile for this eroticised bird-woman embrace. Sometimes Lee is closer. 'So heavy passion then rests' is, like the Latin original, almost impossible to understand, whereas Green has diverged further from Catullus in the attempt to make his version intelligible. Where Green imitates the poetic metre of the original – producing a rhythm that may be difficult for English-speaking readers to hear as metre at all – Lee naturalises or domesticises the poetic form, rendering the hendecasyllables of the Latin into an audibly rhythmical trochaic tetrameter.

But perhaps the most important difference of technique between the two translations is that Lee relies heavily on English cognates of the Latin words that he translates: 'small solace' for the diminutive *solacium*, 'cares' for *curas*, 'desire' for *desiderium*. While not going all the way towards homophony in the Zukofsky mode, Lee incorporates numerous words that sound like Latin, because they come from Latinate roots. But the Romans did not use Latinate language. They used Latin, which was not always a dead language. Latinisms in English often sound stiff and over-educated; there is no reason to think that the Latin of Catullus consistently felt this way to the Romans. In Green's version, by contrast, the diminutive comfort of *solacium* becomes 'just a smidgin of … comfort,' *desiderium* is 'longing', and *curae* are 'depression'. One could quibble that 'smidgin' is a dated colloquialism, and that 'depression' suggests a modern concept of mental health that would have been unfamiliar to the ancients. But a different kind of fidelity is represented by Green's willingness to find a modern English equivalent, rather than parroting the original with Latinate words – when those Latin words themselves would not immediately have sounded pompous to a Roman reader or listener. If he uses a Latinism (such as 'incandescent', or even, in poem 5, '*ad infinitum*'), it almost never mimics the Latin of the Latin.

Classicists sometimes complain that Green is a 'free' translator, because he occasionally glosses or skips references that the average modern reader might find obscure, and because his versions are racier, slangy, and more fun to read than most of their competitors. Readers who want a more strait-laced Catullus may be happier with the revised Loeb (by Goold). But it is a mistake to think that more vanilla versions of any classical poet are more faithful to the original in every respect, especially when the original is as lively and varied as the poetry of Catullus. As in all translation, every accuracy comes with another kind of betrayal. In poem 2, for example, the Loeb rendition of the opening takes us to a slightly archaic, almost faux-Tudor world: 'Sparrow, my lady's pet, with whom she often plays whilst she holds you in her lap'. This weirdly lumbering set of words conveys the general sense of Catullus's Latin, but gives no hint of the playful sassiness or artful rhythms of the original. 'My lady' introduces a note of performative archaism that is a world away from the Latin *puella*.

Puella is an essential word both in Catullus and in later Latin elegists such as Propertius and Ovid, and is the ordinary Latin word for 'girl'. But it is also used for the poet's mistress or girlfriend (words with very different connotations in English), and for a young woman who might or might not be married. Catullus uses the movingly stark but resonant phrase in the middle of poem 8: *uale, puella*. One could translate this, as Guy Lee does, 'Goodbye, girl'. This has a nice pop-song simplicity. But the neutrality of 'girl' misses the suggestion that Catullus is saying goodbye to the woman he loves, his sexual partner and beloved; it misses, too, the implication that this is an attempted farewell to the seductions of femininity. Moreover, *puella* may have much less positive connotations. Catullus could be saying, 'Farewell, darling', but he could also be saying, 'Good riddance, whore'. Peter Green gives us a gentle dismissal: 'So goodbye, sweetheart'. But elsewhere in Green, a *puella defututa* is 'that fucked-out little scrubber'. Green's translation rightly reminds us that the connotations of the Latin word run all the way from 'sweetheart' to 'scrubber'.

A translator who tries to find 'neutral' language – as if there were such a thing – may take a greater liberty with the original than one who casts their linguistic net as wide as it will go. Literalism brings its own distortions. Consider the first words of Catullus's *libellus* (little booklet), as rendered by the Loeb translation: 'To whom am I to present my pretty new book, freshly smoothed off with dry pumice-stone?' This rendering is perfectly accurate. It conveys the general gist of the lines; every word in the original is translated; there are no obvious interpolations of extra material. It would do well as a crib to help those with nascent or rusty Latin struggle through the original. What it does not do is give any indication of what the original feels like. The Loeb translation is not poetry, or even verse. It does not convey Catullus's stylistic carefulness, his wit, his comic self-deprecation or his consciousness of Hellenistic literary antecedents – all of which are apparent in the original. 'Literal' translation may make Catullus sound like a clumsy writer, or an artless one – when nothing can be further from the truth. Catullus brought into written Latin the spoken voices of the bedroom and the street. He is full of colloquialisms, slang, dirty words, puns, neologisms, diminutives and jokes. He shifts with unnerving speed between elevated poetic language and conversational Latin. He was criticised in his own time for stylistic originality: Catullus and his circle were known to Cicero by the derogatory nicknames 'New Poets' or 'Innovators' (*poetae novi* or neoterics). A translation that presents Catullus as a poet with a bland, unvarying style and a limited vocabulary will be highly misleading.

There are many conventional metaphors for translation that make it sound fairly straightforward. Translators are often said to 'carry over' a piece of work from one language to another, or dress it up in new clothes, or pour it into a new vessel. They must choose, in the Ciceronian cliché, between translating 'word for word' and 'sense for sense'. But translation, perhaps especially the translation of poetry, is never really so simple. Meaning, form and language are intertwined. A poem belongs to the culture in which it was produced; sense is not separable from particular words, their rhythms, their connotations, their history.

One approach to this fundamentally insoluble problem is to try to produce a version that is as lively as the original, even if this means importing concepts that are obviously modern and unclassical. Sir John Denham, the seventeenth-century poet and classical translator, convincingly remarked that a poetic translator's business is not merely to translate 'Language into Language, but Poesie into Poesie; and Poesie is of so subtile a spirit, that in pouring out of one Language, into another, it will all evaporate; and if a new spirit be not added in the transfusion, there will remain nothing but a *Caput mortuum*, there being certain Graces and Happinesses peculiar to every Language, which gives life and energy to the words'.

But this does not end the matter: there are several very different possible approaches available for a translator who hopes to generate a new spirit, to give 'life and energy' to their work. One approach is to write in a way that, as far as possible, masks the translation's status as a translation. Heidegger said that 'the good translator disappears from view, even while preserving the text'. Many translators of ancient poetry before the twentieth century adopt versions of this approach. Ben Jonson's translation of Catullus's poem 5 – 'Come, my Celia, let us prove / while we may, the sports of love' – is both a translation and an original composition (and also a song lyric used in Jonson's original satirical comedy, *Volpone*). But reminders of the translator's presence may allow for a different kind of fidelity to different truths: that our own culture is very different from that of ancient Rome, and the English language is different – in its morphology, syntax, connotations, and in its ways of dividing and conceptualising reality – from Latin. English has a far larger lexicon than extant classical Latin: the most recent *Oxford English Dictionary* includes over 600,000 words, whereas the *Oxford Latin Dictionary* has entries for only 40,000. But it does not necessarily follow that English speakers can express fifteen times the number of thoughts and emotions that were available to the Romans. It may be that Latin speakers, like Lewis Carroll's Humpty Dumpty, made each of their words work harder than most English words do.

There are many viable ways to interpret and recreate the poetry of Catullus for readers of English. A defensible approach to the lively, astonishingly varied poetic oeuvre of Catullus is simply to ignore most of its stylistic playfulness and artifice, and render it all in strange prose – as the Loeb translation does. Another defensible approach is to use polished but fairly neutral language, and recognisably anglophone poetic forms, like Guy Lee. It is also justifiable to do as Peter Green does: to imitate the alien poetic metres of the Latin, while also channelling Catullus's striking combination of high and low diction, of the literary with the chatty, into a fun, strange combination of high diction and emotional melodrama (those 'incandescent longings') with a brave use of slang, both British and American ('jack off', 'prick', 'cute', 'asshole', 'dumbass', 'fuckwits', 'a backwoods hick', 'hotshots', 'dishy', 'neat', 'shack up'). Isobel Williams's *Switch* (2023) goes much further in this direction: her Catullus features polyester, Gucci earrings,

Coke and Doritos, vindaloo and digital currency – and the translations/imitations are juxtaposed with line drawings suggesting Japanese rope bondage. Williams' magpie linguistic inventiveness takes us to worlds very distant from Catullus's Rome – yet it also provides a suggestive image of how Catullus might have written, if he'd lived in the twenty-first century (which the Loeb translation certainly does not).

In the turbulent last days of the Roman Republic, art and personal relationships offered at least a 'smidgen of comfort' from the cares generated by political and social upheaval. The poetry of Catullus evokes love, desire and the experiences of being young and in love. But as the versions by Anne Carson, Peter Green and Isobel Williams all show in different ways, Catullus's work is also about language, bafflement, grief, rage and comedy, and an obsessive, perhaps futile desire for control. Like the furious young lover in his eternal longing for an inaccessible, repeatedly unfaithful object of desire, the translators themselves strive for a voice or style that might be able to achieve the impossible, or dominate the indomitable – or at the very least, articulate the eternal experience of frustration.

CHILL OUT WITH THE STOICS

Stoicism is having a moment. Ryan Holiday and Stephen Hanselman's *The Daily Stoic* (2016) has been a bestseller in the Business Motivation, Success Self-Help, and Greek and Roman Philosophy categories – despite, or perhaps because of, its simplistic self-importance. Holiday – formerly a marketer for American Apparel – is one of many current motivators and influencers promoting a revised version of ancient Stoicism as the best way to achieve calm in our current age of anxiety. Stoicism offers an important example of how contemporary people may claim ideas from Greek and Roman antiquity to serve modern cultural imperatives.

The presence of massive and ever-increasing economic inequality, combined with the rise of autocracy and growing political disempowerment even for the very rich, are features that contemporary US and UK societies share with the ancient periods in which Stoicism was most popular. It is a philosophical and psychological system designed to comfort the rich and powerful for any perceived limits on their power, by assuring them that they are, after all, in control of everything that matters. It also conveniently promotes an idea of 'virtue' that is compatible with ignoring or enabling the suffering of everyone else in the world.

Stoicism was founded in Athens by Zeno in the fourth century BCE as a version of the philosophy of Socrates. It developed and flourished for at least another 500 years, well into the later Roman Empire. The last major ancient Stoic-influenced writer was the emperor Marcus Aurelius (121–180 CE), whose *Meditations* amply demonstrate his deep engagement with the philosophy that he learned with Rusticus, his tutor.

Ancient Stoicism, and its modern capital-S reinventions, is not identical with small-s 'stoicism' in the modern sense, although the concepts overlap. A modern 'stoic' is a person who puts up with pain or suffering without complaining, without expressing any sign of emotion. The Stoics, by contrast, did not aim at emotional repression but at retraining our emotional responses. They thought that one could achieve a state of consciousness such that the things most people mind about – such as physical pain, and all the things that usually cause us anger, grief, frustration and so on – would no longer feel important. The point is not to pretend that sickness, death and dishonour do not exist, or to deny the facts of loss, as in modern positive thinking. Instead, a true Stoic would be genuinely unaffected by such external losses. In modern terms, your lost job and lost career prospects, your now worthless pension plan, your professional and social humiliation and isolation, your bankruptcy, your foreclosed home, your cancerous breasts, your dead children – all are, from a Stoic perspective, 'indifferent' – they are at most, 'not preferable'. What matters, in good times or bad, is not whether you have a job, an income, a family, or a home, but whether you have the inner strength to realise how little such things matter.

The Stoics taught that reason is the guiding force of the world, and ought to be the guiding principle of each human being. Thinking, and trying our best to discover the truth about the universe as well as about human life, is part of our duty as Stoics. Rather than shut our eyes to the truth, we must work to make it acceptable emotionally. Everything happens for a reason, and if we could only align our feelings and actions with our reason and with the forces of the universe – 'live in accordance with Nature', as the Stoic slogan had it, or 'want what is' – we could live a life of perfect virtue and, hence, perfect tranquillity.

The desire for peace of mind is common among people of all social classes, not only the very rich and powerful. One of the most important ancient teachers of Stoicism, the first-century CE Stoic philosopher and teacher, Epictetus, was an enslaved person who succeeded in getting an education and, eventually, his freedom. Images of freedom, slavery and self-belonging (*oikoiēsis*) recur in his teaching. 'A slave is always praying to be set free', he writes. He evokes the horrors of enslavement by describing the suffering of caged animals and birds that refuse to eat in captivity and starve to death, though he also occasionally repeats a conventional set of ideas about slavery, claiming, for example, that runaway slaves are 'cowards', and that none of them ever dies of hunger.

Slavery powered the Roman Empire; in the first century CE, between 10 and 20 per cent of the population were enslaved at any one time. But Epictetus was not an abolitionist in a political sense. Like other ancient philosophers, he assumed that slavery was normal and would always exist. He never suggests that those who claimed to own their fellow human beings were committing a moral evil. His aim was to free others from the 'tyrannic sway' not of literal enslavers, but of the emotional disturbance caused by false belief.

For Epictetus, even an enslaved person can be 'free', through the alignment of their will with nature and the universe. He quotes with admiration a line from Diogenes the Cynic, who was taken captive but still considered himself free, thanks to his philosophical teacher: 'Slavery became a thing of the past for me after Antisthenes set me free.' According to one story, Epictetus's enslaver asked him if he wanted to be set free. 'Why?' Epictetus replied. 'Do you think I am in any way bound?' In another story the enslaver twisted Epictetus's leg so aggressively that he warned his tormentor that the bone might break. The enslaver continued to twist and the leg snapped. Epictetus said calmly: 'I told you you would break it.' A tyrant can claim your leg, remove your head or kill your family. 'What can't be chained or removed?' Epictetus asked, and answered his own question: 'Your will.'

Ancient biographical traditions are not known for their factual accuracy, and some of the anecdotes about Epictetus's life in slavery may be embellishments. He seems to have walked with a limp in later life; perhaps this was caused by the enslaver's mistreatment, or perhaps the story was invented to explain the limp. The chief outlines of his life are clear. He was born into slavery around the middle of the first century CE in Hierapolis ('Holy City'), in modern Turkey. He was Greek, or at least spoke the language fluently from an early age. At some point he was sold to a powerful Roman, Tiberius Claudius Epaphroditus, and taken to Rome, probably soon after the suicide of Nero in 68 CE. Despite being enslaved, Epictetus attended philosophical lectures. Around 79 CE, when he was in his late twenties, he would have been able to hear the teaching of the Stoic philosopher Musonius Rufus, who welcomed everybody, even women and enslaved men. A year or so later, Epictetus was set free from enslavement and became a philosophy teacher himself. He probably left Rome during the reign of Domitian, who forced philosophy teachers out of the city on suspicion of anti-imperial sympathies. He moved to Nicopolis in western Greece, where he continued to teach for the remainder of his long life. He died around 130 CE.

Epictetus was a teacher, not a writer. His life's work was to liberate his students and interlocutors from false beliefs and the tyranny of passion. He had no interest in philosophical originality or in crafting elegant sentences that would preserve his name forever, and his version of Stoicism did not concentrate on technical debates about logic, physics or metaphysics (core subjects for other Stoic thinkers). He spent his days talking to people. But one of his many students, Arrian (famous also for his account of the eastern campaigns of Alexander the Great), wrote what he described as a verbatim record of Epictetus's teaching in four books, known as the *Discourses*. He also wrote a separate summary of it, known as the *Handbook*.

A short, accessible pamphlet, the *Handbook* (*Encheiridion* in Greek) has been the more popular and widely read of the two texts and can readily serve as a very short introduction to Stoicism. But you need to read the more expansive *Discourses* to understand the charm of Epictetus's version of the philosophy, which depends not on the regurgitation of Stoic doctrine but on the vigorous, humane and often funny interaction of the teacher with his students, and his insights into the concerns that impede their philosophical progress. The *Discourses* are not easy to read straight through because there is no real structure or development, but they are wonderful to dip into. (The same is true of Marcus Aurelius's *Meditations*, to which we'll turn in a moment).

Stoicism was a well-established philosophical system by Epictetus's time. Founded by Zeno and developed by Chrysippus, Stoicism included logic and physics as well as 'ethics' – a set of teachings about the disposition and behaviour needed to attain well-being. The modern term 'ethics' may be a little misleading as a descriptor of the ancient field: Stoic ethics was concerned not with establishing a rational basis for moral judgements, but with the way an individual – usually imagined as a male, relatively privileged individual – could attain the best possible life, through making himself immune to the vicissitudes of fortune. The goal was 'well-being' – *eudaimonia* – a term that is sometimes misleadingly translated as 'happiness': for a Stoic, as for an Epicurean or a Cynic, well-being is not about feeling cheerful, but about control. The philosopher seeks *ataraxia*: a state of being untroubled, which could be attained by ridding yourself of false beliefs and aligning yourself with what truly matters.

According to the Epicureans, the true good is pleasure, of a moderate, balanced kind. For the Stoics, by contrast, the true good is individual human excellence or virtue – *aretē* in Greek, or *virtus* in Latin. Such excellence, for the Stoics, could be attained only by aligning your own will with the universe, nature, fate, or God (the Stoics often spoke of a singular deity). The central theme in the teaching of Epictetus is that we can and must choose to stop paying attention to things we have no control over. 'Some things are up to us and some are not', the *Handbook* begins – foreshadowing the teachings of modern recovery programmes and the Serenity Prayer, with its distinction between the things we can change and the things we cannot.

For Epictetus, nothing is up to us except our own purpose, attitude or 'will', as Robin Waterfield puts it in his translation from 2022 (the Greek is *prohairesis*): 'Wealth, health, status – these things aren't up to us.' Rhetorically, it's no coincidence that these lists of unimportant things – there are many of them in the teachings of Epictetus – tend to focus on individual privileges that most people would agree are overvalued. An ancient Roman student or reader, even one entirely innocent of philosophy, would not be surprised to learn that it is undignified to be too concerned with money or prestige, or that the bravest, most noble man will show courage in the face of physical danger. Epictetus presents a version of Stoicism that generally aligns with traditional Roman social norms, even if his expression of those ideals is wonderfully precise and memorable. 'I'll cut off your head', a tyrant threatens. 'Well,' the Stoic replies, 'have you ever heard me suggest that I'm unique in having a non-detachable head?' Robin Waterfield's readable translation brings out Epictetus's humour and conversational tone as well as his philosophical vision. In another episode from the *Handbook*, a preening man comforts himself with the thought: 'I have gorgeous hair.'

In terms of behaviour, too, Epictetus's version of Stoicism posed no threat to existing social norms. Diogenes the Cynic had shown his contempt for convention by living in a barrel, wearing rags and defecating in public, but Epictetus recommends that his students adapt themselves with dignity to perform whatever social role they find themselves inhabiting. This is not a philosophy to inspire a slave revolt, or a revolution. All anger – including righteous rage at collective injustice – is to be eradicated for the individual's peace of mind. The followers of Epictetus are supposed to do what is 'appropriate' (*kathēkon*), and he does not worry about defining or reimagining what that might be. Convention and tradition are good enough guides. According to Epictetus, the Epicurean ideal of a quiet life focused on friendship and moderate pleasure is 'subversive of the state, destructive of households and unsuitable even for women', but Stoicism will allow an elite Roman man eager to advance in his political career to perform his normal 'duties'.

Presumably, most of the students of Epictetus were privileged men; the anonymous addressee is always imagined as masculine. The philosophical learner implied by the text is usually a wealthy, privileged enslaver, whose problems include such trivialities as 'the slave' bringing water that isn't hot enough. Epictetus advises the student who has been 'assigned a somewhat higher station' in life to be 'just' and 'decent' in his response (qualities that are viewed as quite compatible with enslaving other humans). At the same time, however, he pushes back against the idea, present in ancient philosophical thought since at least the time of Aristotle, that some human beings are naturally slavish. The enslaved are the enslaver's kinsmen, Epictetus says, and they, too, are the offspring of Zeus; their subjugation is not justified by their supposed inferiority. The only real 'slaves' are those who have failed to follow Stoic teaching – including the philosopher's ostensibly free students. He hammers this point home by addressing the reader who is subject to the whims of passion as 'Slave!'

The central distinction between what is and what is not 'up to us' (*eph'hēmin*) relies, in Epictetus's work, on an individualistic idea of human motivations and values. What is 'up to us' tends to mean 'what is up to me'. There is no possibility of collective action. Some Roman Stoics and Stoic-sympathisers were closely associated with opposition to imperial rule and a desire to return to the old days of the Republic. Political revolution can be 'up to us' only collectively: it usually takes more than one person to topple an imperial regime. But a revolutionary desire for political reform is not a feature of Epictetus's version of Stoicism. 'It's not poverty that we need to get rid of,' he says, 'but our judgement of poverty.' The context is not poverty as a social evil, but advice to a young man who wants his father to give him a larger allowance.

This is the kind of problem that Epictetus's version of Stoicism is designed to address: a privileged man is disturbed by the idea that he does not have complete control over every element of his existence. Epictetus's teaching intervenes from two different directions. It knocks the egotistical student down a peg or two ('Slave!'), while providing a philosophically authorised justification for his fantasies of power, permanence and autonomy.

Historically, the most powerful of all Stoics was the perennially fascinating Marcus Aurelius, Roman emperor and author of the Stoic-infused *Meditations* – his jottings and notes-to-self, on philosophy and the meaning of life. The *Meditations* are a favourite of Bill Clinton's, and they are, like the works of Epictetus, an oft-cited inspiration to many powerful people in politics and business today. Would the world be a better place if all world leaders were Stoics?

The question seems particularly relevant at the moment, since Marcus Aurelius faced problems that recall many of the largest global issues we face today. His rule endured a severe economic crisis; a growing gulf between rich and poor; a series of apparently endless, costly, bloody and controversial wars in multiple corners of a sprawling, unmanageable empire; new plagues bringing death and terror to the domestic population; a culture increasingly addicted to violent and mindless forms of entertainment; and growing religious fanaticism, including the presence of a new cult that encouraged its members to martyr themselves for their cause. It all sounds darkly familiar. Was his Stoicism a help or a hindrance in managing these social and political dilemmas?

Marcus spent most of his last decade, until his death in 180 CE, out in barbarian territory, warring against the Germanic tribes in the west to defend the outer boundaries of his sprawling empire. He seems to have believed that violence, cruelty and enslavement were justifiable, so long as they were in the service of Rome. He was fundamentally a Roman patriot. Although he urges himself to act as a 'citizen of the universe', Rome was far more than just one place in the world. It was an idea, and one which was intimately connected with Marcus's sense of his dignity and his integrity. 'Every hour, give vigorous attention, as a Roman and as a man, to the performance of the task at hand.' For him, as for many other Stoic-minded Romans, the interrelated qualities of being male and being Roman lay at the heart of what he was most proud of in himself. The strong, masculine virtue (*virtus* is literally 'masculinity') of the Roman and of the Stoic sage are treated as one.

The *Meditations* were composed while on campaign. They say almost nothing explicitly about contemporary events, but they are full of references to disease, to war, to anger and conflict, to death. Marcus had been made emperor at only seventeen; the *Meditations* provide a glimpse of how stressful and often enraging this most privileged of career paths could be.

Stoicism, unlike its most prominent rival philosophical tradition, Epicureanism, did not advocate for withdrawal from public life. But Stoicism was not primarily designed to guide the public man in his public actions. Rather, its goal, not always achieved, was to enable him to experience their vicissitudes and horrors with equanimity. Stoicism is not designed to make the world a better place, nor even to nurture kindness in the individual Stoic. Rather, it is a philosophy designed to help individuals, especially very privileged individuals, align themselves with the universe as it already exists, and thereby shore up their sense of their own unassailable strength and importance, even in the face of pain, trouble and death.

How should we think about the surging popularity of Stoicism in the US, and broader Anglo and European worlds, in the twenty-first century? Like monotheistic religious traditions, Stoicism and Neo-Stoicism offer the comforting promise of being able, perhaps, one day, to live a good life, and find some kind of peace amid the chaos and fear of uncertain times. But more than many of these, Stoicism also offers the allure of three other ideals: rationality, power and masculinity. In the anglophone world, important people in business and tech are sometimes leery of the devoted, abject faith required by many monotheistic traditions. Other philosophical and religious traditions encourage their followers to aspire to an emptiness of the self, mirroring the emptiness of reality (in Sanskrit, *sūnyatā*) or the self-emptying of God (in Greek, *kenōsis*). In Stoicism, the self is always the focus, even for the most enlightened philosopher. The wise Stoic never gives up his desire for power and possessions, goals that can be achieved through control over the will. This feature helps explain why Stoicism, in a watered-down form, is currently so popular with wealthy people, mostly white men, in Silicon Valley or Wall Street. It is a spiritual path for people who want to hold on to their sense of self and their own power.

Stoicism provides a great deal of useful guidance for life, even for those of us who are neither ancient Roman citizens nor entrepreneurs. It may be helpful for coping with the annoyance, frustration and boredom of daily life. 'If you're going out to bathe,' Epictetus says, 'rehearse in your mind what typically happens in a bathhouse – getting splashed and jostled and abused and robbed.' This is a good principle to bear in mind if your train or plane is delayed by several hours and then cancelled. It can be soothing to remember that there is nothing unusual about such occurrences, which are beyond your control, allowing you to stay calm and align your will with that of the universe.

Stoicism can help with physical pain, too. During a recent bout of searing back pain that left me unable to walk, I found it genuinely helpful to remember that I had a choice about how to respond to my pain and my physical immobility: I could choose not to 'consider my body to be mine', not to be sorry for myself, or frightened, or angry, and to think of myself, or at least of my 'command centre' (as

Waterfield translates the 'leading element' of the self, *to hēgemonikon*), as both free and powerful, even when I could barely move.

The teachings of Stoicism are rather less useful when it comes to interactions with other people. 'If you kiss a child of yours,' Epictetus says, 'or your wife, tell yourself that you're kissing a human being, because then you won't be upset if they die.' This must have been a common piece of Stoic advice; the line is quoted admiringly by Marcus Aurelius. But such mantras are not much good if you consider your children's well-being more important than your own tranquillity. Epictetus discusses the case of a man who leaves home when his child is sick because he cannot bear to contemplate her suffering or the possibility of her death. He concedes that this is not the most 'affectionate' thing to do: if the mother and enslaved caregivers had done the same, the child would have been left entirely alone. He does not explain why these people stay to take care of the child, although it's probably that they were more concerned with the child's needs than their own feelings – and also that, as subordinates, they had little or no choice in the matter. As a model for political leadership, the story is not reassuring: I personally would not prefer to live in a society whose most powerful members were constantly training themselves to be indifferent to everyone else's suffering or imminent death. For all the vigorous imagery and macho tough-mindedness, it is hard to avoid the suspicion that Stoicism can easily serve to authorise a fancy, rationalised form of egotism.

The case of ancient Stoicism provides a powerful

cautionary tale against the idea that we should treat ancient culture as a repository of unambiguously valuable 'wisdom' for the modern age. We should instead look back to ancient philosophy and ancient poetry for deeper understanding of human possibilities, and as sparks for new forms of insight and creativity – without imagining that anyone, including the ancient philosophers, had all the answers about how to live.

WAR MUSIC

Some of the most interesting reinventions of ancient literature have been created by non-classicists, who may be able to approach the material with the fresh eyes of an outsider. Perhaps the most powerful example is Christopher Logue's *War Music* – a powerful poetic reimagining of the *Iliad* that manages to bring the vivid similes and divine epiphanies of the Greek original to a startling, dazzling new life.

As a child, Logue had a habit of petty theft. In his memoir, *Prince Charming*, he reveals that he stole money from his parents, then sweets from the local shop, and later pornographic magazines. He once robbed a little girl of her ice cream at toy-gun-point – a crime that resulted in his being sent miserably away to boarding school. But perhaps the most characteristic of Logue's boyhood crimes was that he secretly wrote his own name at the end of a fair copy he made of Rudyard Kipling's poem, 'Gunga Din', as if he himself were the author. Logue went on to make a wonderfully idiosyncratic literary career founded on the practice of poetic theft. The biggest and most extraordinary heist is his haunting, capricious patchwork of poetic narratives based on Homer's *Iliad* – a grand larceny made all the more extraordinary by the fact that the thief knew no Greek at all, so he should have had no way to break into the crypt. Virgil, so legend has it, was accused of stealing from Homer when he began work on the *Aeneid*. He replied that it is easier to steal Hercules' club than to steal a line from Homer. Any hack versifier can write Audenesque pontifications, but it is a tall order to remake Homer into a contemporary idiom, and Christopher Logue seemed, on the face of it, entirely ill-equipped for this mission impossible.

He came from a modest background (his father was a post office worker), and he had no university education (though he liked the idea of Oxford in theory). After an unhappy and alienated adolescence in an Irish Catholic boarding school, where he was disliked and beaten (Logue was a lifelong atheist) and performed fairly badly academically, he joined the army, lacking any better ideas about what to do with his life. At the end of his service, he was court-martialled and imprisoned for two years, for possession of stolen pay books. The crime seems to have been a half-conscious attempt to get himself kicked out of the army, in what he himself describes as a mixture of masochism and spite.

Logue's life after prison was peripatetic. He spent some years in Paris, and made friends with various eminent literary people, including the elderly Beckett. On his return to England, he became active in the nascent campaign against nuclear arms, and was briefly imprisoned. He published poems in journals like the *TLS* and in a couple of books, churned out a pornographic novel, *Lust* (for which he was paid $1 a page), wrote some screenplays, adapted Pablo

Neruda's 'Twenty Love Poems' and combined them with a jazz track by Tony Kinsey on the wonderful record 'Red Bird', and appeared in several films as an actor, including as Cardinal Richelieu in Ken Russell's *Devils*.

One of Logue's main life goals was to avoid anything like an actual job. He succeeded, and his ramshackle series of projects, whims, friendships and fads all seem to have played their part in the construction of his major work of literary plunder, which has, at times, a jazzy rhythm, an improvisatory feel, a cinematic sensibility, awkwardness, an ambiguous, perhaps incoherent attitude towards war, a fetishistic love of detail, some idiosyncratic silliness, and a willingness to pause at odd moments and notice the unexpected.

Logue died in 2011, with the Homer project still not quite finished. But finishing was never really the point, since Logue takes little hints and nuggets here and there from Homer – he never aims for a complete retelling. The various volumes, along with the fragments of an ending, were eventually published together in 2016 as *War Music*, tastefully edited by the poet Christopher Reid. The collection includes an Appendix of Logue's notes towards the final volume, 'Big Men Falling a Long Way', which consists of 'fragments' based on books 10–24, and ends with the meeting of Priam and Achilles, from *Iliad* book 24.

War Music is Logue's Homer in as complete a state as it will ever be, and it is cause for celebration. Logue's individual volumes, published earlier, have been bombastically hailed as 'the best translation of Homer since Pope's' (Gary Wills), and the word 'genius' has been bandied around by several critics, including George Steiner. Logue's 'account' of Homer is imperfect, but it has far more moments of startling brilliance than anybody could reasonably expect. Logue had no particular interest in Homer until he was asked by the classicist and translator Donald Carne-Ross in 1959 to produce a readable script version of *Iliad* book 16 for the BBC. *War Music* is not in any obvious sense a 'translation' of the *Iliad*, although it has a close relationship with it. Logue worked from existing translations and from cribs created for him by Carne-Ross.

Logue himself called it 'my Homer poem' or 'an account of the *Iliad*'; he wanted to create a poem that was 'dependent' on Homer, but with a larger aim – to 'revitalize narrative verse'. Logue's *Music* does indeed have a music, based primarily on an iambic pentameter line, often broken up by shorter phrases by the effective use of line breaks. His work in film shows to powerful effect in the way he cuts between scenes, setting us instantly in one place, then changing the shot – a technique that allows for authentically Homeric sudden shifts between the worlds of gods and mortals:

> And with a wish He turned the fog to light,
> And with a word He called them back to Heaven.
> Sky.
> Snow.
> The 1000 yards.
> The palisade.
> Hector: 'I am your Prince'.

The gulf between worlds is marked by a shift in verse form, and a change in the layout of the page – techniques that are, of course, absent from Homeric hexameter, which always scans the same way and implies no page on which to lie. But in his use of the sudden turn, the combination of speed and repetition, and the simple visual cues to shape a story, Logue makes us feel that he is in touch with some deep elements of the source text.

Logue's quick-cutting technique also allows for heart-stopping shifts between different time periods, a mode that again is at least reminiscent of Homer: 'Go back an hour. / See what the Mousegod saw.' The Iliadic narrative is concentrated on a short episode in a long war, but it zips back and forth in time, recalling, for instance, the original abduction of Helen in her re-abduction in Book 3, and anticipating the fall of the city in the final death of Hector. We are constantly reminded of the painful, chilling gap between the moments inhabited briefly by mortals, and the longer scope of time that is visible to the gods'-eye view of the world. Andromache prepares hot baths for Hector, not knowing that he is already dead. Helen looks from the wall of Troy for her brothers, not knowing that they are already in the 'grain-giving' earth of Sparta. Logue often reaches for this mode, as in the scene from Book 3, where Hector proposes a duel with Menelaus:

> 'And if I die' (this said within an inch of where he
>   will)
> 'My corpse belongs to Troy and to Andromache'.

The notion that a dead body is a thing that belongs to anyone (rather than being a person, to be treated honourably) is an anachronism, as is the notion of 'my corpse' (rather than 'myself'): the Homeric dead are people, not husks of people. But the brevity of the parenthesis packs a Homeric punch. Sometimes Logue spells out this kind of resonant gap, as he does with Helen's dead brothers: Helen thinks of them pulling off her covers in bed,

> and imagines that Troy is only a dream:
> But Troy was not a dream, and they lay dead,
> Killed by their neighbours in a hillside war,
> Beneath the snowy sheep that graze on Sparta.

This is far more detail about the brothers' death and about Helen's state of mind than we are given by the Homeric original. But there is something unexpectedly Homeric in the temporal and spatial confusion, the glimpse of a world opening up, to acknowledge that Troy is not the only war, and that wars may be entirely trivial, fought on a 'hillside' for no reason worth mentioning.

The most obvious way that Logue jumps across the passage of time is in his use of flagrantly anachronistic similes. These are sometimes gimmicky, and they do not always come off: 'blood like a car-wash' feels oddly predictable (there are too many car park and car-wash references in Logue); 'as many arrows on his posy shield / As microphones on politicians' stands' takes one in a tedious direction, as does the idea that looking into God's eyes ('when he is cross') is 'like running into searchlights turned full on'. Sometimes the modern references feel as if Logue has lost the plot; we do not need to be told that men crammed together in battle are 'like shoppers', or to have a reference to 'Miss Heber's Diary, 1908'. A sequence of references to later celebrities in battle (Richard III on Bosworth field, Marshal Ney under Napoleon) meanders through some dates and numbers culled from biographical sources ('July 4th to 14th '43, 700 tanks engaged'), to end up with 'Back to today' – er, yes please.

But for the most part, the anachronistic similes are extraordinarily powerful. As Hector steps out to fight (and, in Logue's condensed time scheme, to his imminent death), the Greek army responds as one:

> Think of a raked sky-wide Venetian blind.
> Add the receding traction of its slats
> Of its slats of its slats as a hand draws it up.
> Hear the Greek army getting to its feet:
> Then of a stadium when many boards are raised
> And many faces change to one vast face.
> So, where there were so many masks,
> Now one Greek mask glittered from strip to ridge.

The terrifying use of ordinary experience to describe something extraordinary feels reminiscent of Homer, and Logue's imagery, like Homer's, suggests more than one point of comparison. Later, Logue manages to give us a dispassionate glimpse of Patroclus piercing a victim with his spear and hoisting him up from the throng of bodies, 'As easily as later men / Disengage a sardine from a tin'. The original simile invokes a man sitting fishing on a rock, hoisting up a big fish on a line. Logue's updated version retains two crucial elements in the source text: the comparison of the scene of human slaughter to an everyday peace-time activity, and the precise visual detail.

Anachronism is fun, and Logue allows one to share his enjoyment in creating a collage made up of pieces from different eras. But it also serves the purpose of not allowing us to think of this story as a distant, musty old classic. Anachronism sucks us in, even when the anachronisms take us all over the modern world:

> It was so quiet in Heaven that you could hear
> The north wind pluck a chicken in Australia.

Logue's story takes place in a setting that is far bigger than that of Homer – big enough to accommodate our modern selves, and to implicate us in some of the most disturbing feelings, like the joy of being a half-naked recruit about to run into battle for one side or another:

> And here it comes:
> That unpremeditated joy as you
> – the Uzi shuddering warm against your hip
> Happy in danger in a dangerous place
> Yourself another self you found at Troy –

Logue convinces us that these selves are indeed part of us, not only by the modern details (the Uzi), but by the authority of the language. By contrast, one of his most annoying tics is the use of exoticising fake-Greek or fake-Aborigine names: Quibuph, T'lesspiax, Neomab, Pagif, Nain, Cumin, Tu, and far too many more. These made-up names locate us nowhere except in Logue's own head, and they make one long for a well-sharpened blue pencil.

Much of Logue's imagery has no particular Homeric antecedent, and the Appendix reveals that he often came up with similes without having a place to stitch them in; they sometimes threaten to take over the narrative, since the imagery can be the most interesting thing happening. Logue has similes within similes, and fluent lists of images that create their own kind of story:

> Consider planes at touchdown – how they poise;
> Or palms beneath a numbered hurricane;
> Or birds wheeled sideways over windswept heights;
> or burly salmon challenging a weir;
> Right-angled, dreamy fliers as they ride
> The instep of a dying wave, or trace
> Diagonals on snowslopes.

The careful account of patterns of motion, and the gradual realisation that the final figures are surfers and skiers, is both beautiful and satisfying – and the supposed point of comparison, Achilles' divine horses galloping across the plain to Troy, is mostly forgotten. Logue sometimes uses

Homer's plot as a hanger on which he can dangle his own lyrical descriptions.

Many of the most powerful passages in *War Music* are not markedly anachronistic, but rely on a close attention to the observable natural world. The narrator assumes that we, like him, have noticed the colours of things, and everything is familiar, until, almost imperceptibly, it becomes disturbingly alien:

> On certain winter days the land seems grey,
> And the no-headroom left between it and the grey
> Masses of downthrust cloud fills with wet haze.
> Lines of cold rain weld mile on sightless mile
> Of waste to air. Floods occupy the state. And still
> The rains continue, grey on grey.

Homer's natural-world similes – the lions, the shepherds, the cranes – operate in something of the same way, juxtaposing an inhuman, 'natural' mode of destruction, with that inflicted on humans by each other. On the other hand, there is a distinctly literary and un-Homeric artistry in Logue's confusing, inverted syntax, and his fondness for surprising buried metaphors ('weld'; 'occupy'). His painterly or cinematic eye for colour has nothing to do with Homer – the Homeric poems, as Gladstone famously pointed out in 1858, have what may seem to modern eyes a strangely limited colour palette. Logue has several brilliant lists of colours, like the one at the start of the *War Music* volume *Pax*: 'Rat. / Pearl. / Onion. / Honey' – a mode of observation that could not be further than Homer's. But it seems pointless to quibble over the ways that Logue's descriptive mode is or is not 'Homeric'. It is good, which matters more. These descriptions locate us in a world that is familiar but that we have never quite seen before, and the sound of words becomes the look of things:

> Blue grey, gold grey, blue gold,
> Translucent nothingnesses
> Readying our space,
> Within the deep, unchanging sea of space,
> For Hesper's entrance, and the silver wrap.

For all his artfulness, Logue also knows the punch that simple words can pack. One of his most famous lyrics from his non-Homeric work is 'Be not too Hard', a ballad which was recorded as a song by Donovan and covered by Joan Baez. Logue's achievement in this deceptively simple poem is to show us the absolute folly of young men who throw away lives that would be short enough anyway – while also reminding us more explicitly of the pointlessness of scolding them. Many of the strongest passages in Logue are apparently simple, authoritative, clearly phrased poetic statements about how the world is, how people are – sometimes in the mouths of the characters, and sometimes spoken by the narrator. Agamemnon declares, 'Never forget that we were born to kill. / We keep the bloodshed to the maximum.' We can see the horror of his perspective more clearly from its propagandistic clarity. These great sententious passages do not create a coherent world view (which is not the point of them), but they create a deep sense of longing for more certainty than the world could ever offer:

> Lord Thoal knows that people love to have a side –
> taking a side as simply as a god.
> And he himself would like to find a god
> who tapped his foot while humans danced.

Logue's master-heist of Homer is combined with many miniature thefts from other poets, and the loot in his commonplace book provides some of the most resonant gnomic utterances. In the first volume, *Kings*, Nestor tells Achilles to back off his quarrel with Agamemnon: 'You are part dust, part deity. / But he is King. And so, for Greece, comes first.' Logue himself acknowledges, in the Eliotesque notes to *Kings*, that the first line here is stolen from Byron's *Manfred*. But there are many other unacknowledged thefts paraded here, not least from Eliot himself, a poet whom Logue adored. Achilles' deathless horses, telling the hero he will die, take on the voice of Eliot's *Four Quartets*: 'This time we will, this time we can, but this time cannot last.' Logue pickpockets from everywhere, high culture and low – from Dryden and Tennyson, to the moment when Achilles, rejecting Nestor's plea for him to return to battle, complains that there has been 'No sign of love for me behind your tears' (a clear allusion to the Paul McCartney song, 'For No One'). When it works – which is surprisingly often, though by no means always – the multiple layers of quotation and allusion create a layered awareness of many moments in time, many pens and typewriters and computers, creating a single, truly epic story.

One might think that the hardest part about rewriting the *Iliad*, for an entirely unbelieving modern poet, would be the presence of the gods. But Logue's divine epiphanies are sometimes astonishingly good. The first moment when Thetis becomes manifest to Achilles, at the start of the volume *Kings*, has a brilliant slow quietness that enables us actually to believe it when we are told how the scent of 'oceanic lavender'

> Drew from the seal-coloured sea onto the beach
> A mist that moved like weed, then stood, then
> turned
> Into his mother, Thetis', lovelost face.

'Lovelost' is a mistake, but the sense of a permeable membrane between two worlds is entirely convincing. More violent divine encounters and descents are often brilliantly done – Athena grabbing Achilles from the quarrel scene, Aphrodite whisking Paris away, or the wonderful sequence in the Patrocleia section when Achilles' friend Patroclus pushes too far ahead, against divine orders, and reaches the wall of Troy. The narrator tells us that he 'fought like dreaming', and his inability to recognise the real divine presence may be half-shared by the reader, until we turn the page and find in a font an inch high: 'APOLLO! Who had been patient with you'. The entirely un-Homeric semantics of typography are enlisted to force the modern reader, just for a moment, to become a total believer in the Olympians.

Apollo and Thetis are far more successfully rendered than the other gods, because Logue allows them to remain as alien beings – Thetis as a manifestation of the sea, and Apollo as the strange 'Mousegod', the brightness of sunlight. It is unfortunate and misleading to make Zeus into 'God', as Logue consistently does, and to suggest that 'He' is infinitely greater than the other deities. The Christianising serves no particular literary purpose, and weakens the more interesting Homeric sense of a world that is full of not one but many inhuman, not fully comprehensible and often hostile beings, whose purposes may contradict one another in unpredictable ways. Worst of all are the depictions of the three main Iliadic goddesses, Athena, Hera and Aphrodite, who are reduced to stereotypes from a sexist TV soap opera – 'The Wife. The Daughter', characterised primarily by their 'creamy' bodies, their 'bums' (there are far too many bums), and their clothes ('both in black wraparound tops'). Athena is 'Teenaged Athena', an epithet that robs her of all power, purpose and strategic skill. Hera is the nagging wife of 'God', 'Greek mad', and bitter that Paris judged her 'less / Nudely speaking'. 'Giggling' Aphrodite ('Miss Tops and Thongs') is rendered mostly by her affinity with 1970s fashion – 'sparkling clogs', 'grey silk lounge pajamas' paired with 'snakeskin flip-flops'. The contrast between the high-stakes world of mortals, and the gods who can afford to be more frivolous, is an essential element of the *Iliad*. But Logue ruins the effect by making us feel that there is nothing to understand about these goddesses – they are made of cardboard. Homer's deities are more than humans only in power, and less than humans only because they have no need of human modes of courage, patience and kindness; they are not less fully realised as people.

But Logue's human people suffer from similar defects, albeit in less glaring ways – especially the female people. The use of the archaism 'a she' to refer to women as prizes of war might have seemed like a way to represent the Homeric elite warriors' commodification of women – but Logue's narrator also sees his women only as 'she's'. Helen, one of the most interesting and complex characters in the Homeric poems, becomes whiny and uninteresting, complaining predictably about her marriage troubles: 'All I do is cry. And that is so annoying.' Indeed it is. The problem, however, is not only that Logue cannot create a convincing female character, but that he has little interest in the experience of any individual character, male or female. He is good at stump-post speeches, but no good at dialogue, no good at grief, and has no deep interest in courage, patience, honour or human interaction. This helps explain why some of the most memorable and emotional moments in the *Iliad* – the tender parting of Hector and Andromache, or the Embassy to Achilles, in which the hero declares that no gifts and no amount of respect could be worth the loss of a single human life, which will never come back once it has crossed the 'barrier of the teeth' – become in Logue flat and forgettable. The choice of Achilles is framed in terms that feel totally unconvincing:

My mother says I have a choice:
Live as a happy backwoods king for aye;
Or give the world an everlasting murmur of my name,
And die.

The awkward, incoherent, and partly archaic phrasing suggests that Logue has not managed to feel his way inside the person who might face a choice like this. The final fragments towards Logue's version of Book 24, the meeting of Achilles with old King Priam, who has come to his enemy's tent to beg for the body of his son from his killer, are equally plodding. The original shows us how desperate the father would have to be to let his lips touch 'the terrible, manslaying hands, that had killed so many of his sons'. Logue's version is simple, but entirely lacking in impact – Achilles lets Priam climb up to him 'and, kneeling, kiss his hands: / The hands that killed his son. / A pause'. It feels hard to care. There are no tears in Logue.

Homer shows us the violence of war, the brevity of human life, and the human yearning to have something that lasts longer – honour, or a place in music and memory. *War Music* has less interest in human grief or human yearnings, and almost no interest in glory; it treats war as a feature of the natural world, or the technological world, which might be the same thing. Individuals – their feelings, their families, their histories, their stories – matter relatively little. What is interesting are the colours, the way things move. This is a strange and surprisingly captivating way of bringing ancient words to life. Logue invites us to watch the Trojan

War as if on a screen, intermittently irritated, but often mesmerised by the surprising beauty of the way the story is told. This is not always a pretty poem, and it is certainly not Homer – but then, smuggling the whole *Iliad* out of the vault of antiquity would have been a tall order. Even if Logue cannot bring us all Homer's treasures, he certainly manages to get some good licks of his ice cream. *War Music* is a powerful achievement, and it invites us to turn back to Homeric poetry with a new eye for what Logue saw in it: the detail that is – like Achilles' divine armour, in Logue's Dylan Thomas-inspired phrase – bright enough to 'scream against the light', and 'so violent it can be seen / Across three thousand years'.

UNWIND THE THREAD

The *Iliad* ends with the funeral laments of three women for the great Trojan warrior, Hector. His wife, Andromache, anticipates the horrors that await her in the wake of her husband's killing: enslavement, a second forced displacement from her home, and the violent death of her baby, who will be hurled from the city walls by the victors. His mother, Hecuba, takes a very different approach, celebrating the glory achieved by a son who died nobly and bravely, in battle. Finally, Helen – once and future wife of the Greek king Menelaus, whose abduction by the Trojan prince, Paris, was the premise for the whole expedition – speaks of her personal grief for a brother-in-law who was kind to her when few others were.

Writing perhaps two hundred years after the composition of the *Iliad* and the *Odyssey*, the Athenian tragic poet Aeschylus is said to have called his plays 'slices from the banquet of Homer'. His great trilogy, the *Oresteia* (composed 458 BCE), returns to questions raised by the end of the *Iliad*: what is the relationship of female grief to male glory? What are the private and familial costs to a great public and military success? And when one side wins, must another always lose?

The *Oresteia* begins with the story of a grieving, righteously angry woman seeking justice for her daughter. The child was killed by her father, the woman's husband, to enable a vast war that enriched himself and his male comrades, and caused devastation to a distant city and its inhabitants, leaving men dead and women grieving. It is, like the *Iliad* and the *Odyssey*, a narrative about the mythical Trojan War, but set in a very different place and time. We begin not on the Trojan plain itself, but in the Greek city of Argos, where Clytemnestra, like Penelope, awaits her long-absent husband – but as we gradually learn, this wife will not welcome the conquering husband back to the marital bed.

Each of the three plays is radically different in style, mood and action. But each centres on female anger and female grief at violent loss of life and the willingness of family members to kill one another. The trilogy is about language and the mysterious will of the gods, about tyranny, freedom and political change, and about a slow path to maturity for one young man (Orestes) and an entire culture. The trilogy plots a shift from a more aristocratic, more mythical, quasi-Homeric world, one of violence, retribution and rage, to a city more like that of Athens in Aeschylus's own time, in which political and legal institutions offer new solutions to the old problems of competing interests and conflict. 'Maturity' turns out to involve the subordination of women and of the family, which is conceived as feminine, to enable the creation of a political community like real-life historical Athens, in which male citizens use the law courts and the institutions of democracy to legislate for structures of power that can contain, marginalise and silence other members of the community – women, immigrants, enslaved people. All the plays' elements are knotted into a central set of questions about how to suppress, silence or pacify female rage, and how to reconcile the close kinship of the household with responsibilities to the larger community or city-state.

In *Agamemnon*, the long first play, the mood is dark and the language is dense, metaphorical and hard to parse. Clytemnestra, Agamemnon's wife, has set up a relay of torch fires to bring her news of her husband's victory at Troy, and the image of the relay signal also connects to the play's larger story: the way events from far away and long ago still haunt the house of Argos. At Aulis, on the way to Troy, Agamemnon was forced to choose between sacrificing his daughter Iphigenia or abandoning the war to recover his brother's wife, Helen – an element of the myth that does not appear in the *Iliad*, perhaps because inter-familial conflict is not what the epic is about. 'Which of these is free from evil?' he asks, in Oliver Taplin's translation (*Oresteia*, 2018). David Mulroy (*Oresteia*, 2018) has the punchier 'Can either choice be right?' Sarah Ruden (in her fine translation in *The Greek Plays*, 2016) makes the phrase more personal: 'But which choice is safe for me?' The Greek original, *ti tōnd' aneu kakōn*, suggests that every kind of badness – from moral evil to personal danger and social humiliation – is associated with this choice. Agamemnon is in a position where there is no right answer, no guiltless or prudent way to act.

The terrible moment is figured as a choice, but one that reduces or eliminates future choices: Agamemnon 'placed his neck beneath the harness / of what had to be' (this and all translations that follow here are by Oliver Taplin unless otherwise noted). The ambiguity of the killer's freedom, or lack of it, is compounded by further mysteries, such as when the cycle of violence began. Was it with the slaughter of Iphigenia? Or longer ago, when Menelaus married Helen, taking a 'lion cub' into his house? Or was it when Atreus, Agamemnon's father, tricked his brother into eating his own children? Or further back still, in the dark plans of Apollo, god of light, and the will of Zeus, 'whoever he may be', the god who killed and usurped his own father? The play's riddling language hints that one word, phrase, action or body can turn into another, often at a terrible price. The death of Iphigenia becomes the death of Agamemnon. More broadly, in one of the Chorus's most powerful images, Ares, the war god, is presented as a money changer who 'trades men into jars' filled with ash. The living become the dead, who in turn haunt the living.

Despite the first play's title, Agamemnon – a flustered, confused, fragile conqueror, who presents himself as a victim even before his wife axes him to death in the bath – plays a relatively small part in it. Two extraordinary female characters dominate its action. Clytemnestra, an intelligent, articulate, determined strategist, is described as a woman whose heart 'organises like a man': she has spent the past ten years plotting her husband's murder, which will allow her (along with her feeble lover, Aegisthus) to seize the throne. Greek tragedy almost never shows violent action; the killing is represented by screams from offstage. But Clytemnestra's triumph over her husband is represented verbally and dramaturgically, above all in the great central scene in which she persuades the reluctant victor to enter the house and trample on the rich red tapestries laid out in his honour, providing a visual acknowledgement that his victory has involved an assumption of infinite privilege ('and who could drain it dry?') and the 'crushing underfoot' of precious things, starting with his own child – 'the treasure of my labour pains', as Clytemnestra puts it. Aeschylus was himself a veteran of the wars in which Athens and other Greek cities fought off attempts at invasion by the Persian army; he is clear-sighted about the greed and egotism of this conquering hero. Clytemnestra hides her intentions in elaborate riddling before the murder, but once her husband is dead, she presents it as orgasmically thrilling: he 'spouted out a jet of blood / that showered me with a drizzle of dark dew', in Taplin's lushly alliterative version. Mulroy has a rather less sexy interpretation of the verb (*ekphysiao*, which suggests 'to snort out' and is used elsewhere for snoring, and elephants squirting water from their trunks): 'He vomited a shining clot of blood.' The combination of 'vomited' with 'shining' feels incoherent: it is unclear why this triumphant murderess would bother to notice how her dead husband's blood catches the light, nor does it seem likely that the blood of a man who has just been hacked to death in the bath would have time to 'clot' before it left his body. Taplin, unlike Mulroy, has understood that Clytemnestra views her husband's violent death not as disgusting ('vomited') but as profoundly satisfying and erotic.

The second great female character in the *Agamemnon* is Cassandra, who seems, on her first entrance, to have a non-speaking role. In 458 BCE, tragedians had only recently begun to use three actors rather than two, and Aeschylus brilliantly exploits the audience's expectations to create surprise and confusion when the third actor, playing the foreign woman enslaved by Agamemnon, speaks. Still more surprising, the outsider turns out to know far more than any native-born Greek about the house of Argos – where, as she well knows, she will die alongside her captor. Queen Clytemnestra's aggression, deceit and violence are counterbalanced by the insight and courage of Cassandra, who is blessed and cursed by Apollo with the gift of prophecy; she sets aside grief for herself and her ruined city to step towards a death that will, as she also knows, bring down her killers.

The Libation Bearers, the middle play of the trilogy, centres on the tomb of the dead Agamemnon and his surviving daughter, Electra. As in the first play, there are contrasting female characters: Electra, driven to murderous plots by long-standing grief and rage, and Clytemnestra, who becomes desperately aware that, like Cassandra before her, she is on the way to death. Electra's brother, Orestes, returns from exile and, urged on by his sister, his friend Pylades and the oracles of Apollo, steels himself to kill his mother and Aegisthus.

These murders parallel those of Agamemnon and Cassandra in the previous play, though they are represented very differently. Clytemnestra luxuriates in the bloody slaughter of her husband, but Orestes hesitates, especially when Clytemnestra bares her breast to remind him that the body he threatens to kill is the source of his life. At the play's end, Orestes presents the murders as an act of political liberation, freeing Argos from a 'pair of tyrants'; but he begins to see visions of the Furies, the doglike, snake-haired goddesses who pursue and torture those who shed the blood of their own family members.

In the final play, *The Eumenides* ('Kindly Ones', a traditional euphemism for the Furies), the goddesses are visible to the audience: they serve as the hissing, violent chorus, in contrast to the human choruses of the first two plays and most other Athenian tragedies. Whereas the earlier plays were set in the distant city of Argos, *The Eumenides* is set where the play was performed: in Athens, on the hill of the Areopagus, a stone's throw from the Theatre of Dionysos. The dominant characters are not humans but gods. Orestes has come to Athens for sanctuary, to beg Athena for absolution from matricide. Athena, like Clytemnestra in *Agamemnon*, is the hyper-intelligent, scheming ruler of her city. But unlike Clytemnestra, she is not mortal, angry, grieving or murderous: she has no personal interest in the case, but turns out to have a particular fondness for the democratic institutions of Athens in the fifth century. She organises a trial by jury.

The Furies accuse Orestes of the ultimate horror in shedding his mother's blood; no matter his justification, they insist that he is polluted and cannot return to Argos or belong to any religious or family community. Apollo speaks in his defence, arguing that matricide does not count as the murder of a family member, because, according to one of several competing medical theories circulating in Aeschylus's time, women's bodies provide only a container for the embryo, which is formed solely of material from the father's body. The jury is split, and Athena breaks the tie in favour of Orestes. Whatever may be true of human biology, she at least is entirely her father's daughter, born from his head: 'And so in every way I'm for the male.' Clytemnestra was accused of having a heart like a man. Electra, in desperate grief, was obsessed with her dead father and absent brother, and resented her mother. Athena takes the pattern of female male-sympathisers even further: she has the militaristic, dominant spirit of her father Zeus, from whose head she emerged after he swallowed her mother (Mētis, 'cunning intelligence'). Athena insists that the sunlit, male-dominated world of politics will, from now on, prevail over the underground, ancestral blood-rights of the female Furies. The Furies are, understandably, furious. But Athena restrains their anger by promising them a permanent, albeit subordinate, place in the ritual life of the city – something analogous to the political status that resident aliens ('metics') had in real-life Athens. The play also provides a mythical, poetic account of how, in real-life fifth century Athens, the Furies came to be worshipped as the "Revered ones" (Semnai) at a sanctuary beneath the Areopagus, and how the Areopagus itself came to be the locus for murder trials.

These dense plays are concerned with a transition from a world of mystery to a world of history, from war to peace, from myth to reality, from aristocratic households to the democratic society of contemporary Athens. They describe the triumph of law over personal vendettas and revenge, and show the direct violence of the axe and the sword giving way to the buried structural violence of law and social institutions. They provide an implicit justification and celebration of recent Athenian history and the current political regime: in real life, the political and legal structures of democracy had replaced the old system of rule by tyrants, and there were still powerful aristocratic men in Athens who favoured oligarchy over democracy. But most fundamentally, the trilogy uses all these interwoven narratives to tell a story that justifies the triumph of men over women. The institution of the all-male democratic law court, presided over by its male-biased judge, is presented as the only possible solution to the endless violence of the earlier, more Homeric world, in which the experiences and voices of angry, wronged, grieving women were allowed to matter as much as those of men. The first two plays show the terrible cost to both men and women of a society in which men favour their bonds with one another over those with their mothers, wives and children. When Agamemnon kills his daughter, his men 'tie a fetter round her / lovely cheeks and face, / a gag to hold her tongue from words to put her / house beneath a curse'. The final play reframes the problem of female suffering by including no women characters: the powerful, immortal Furies are far more menacing than pitiable, and their semi-violent subordination by the goddess Athena, who threatens them with her father's thunderbolt, is presented as the only possible way for the play's vulnerable male human, Orestes, to be saved.

Agamemnon may seem the most mysterious of the three plays; elements that had been only metaphors or dreams in it – hunting dogs, nets, snakes, fire – are summoned from the underworld in the chants of *The Libation Bearers* and become visible on stage in *The Eumenides*, where we see the Furies carrying nets and torches. But in some ways *The Eumenides* is even more abstruse and riddling. Justice – *dikē*, a word that connotes a range of ideas from cosmic balance to moral right, from social custom or judgement to law or the court – shifts in its meanings. In the earlier plays, the rights of one person compete with the rights of another; in *The Eumenides*, Athena answers the Furies' demands for justice (punishment for the male killer, vengeance for his dead female victim) with a judgement based on her own acknowledged bias, and an appeal to Persuasion, the goddess who presides over legislation, not morality. Orestes is acquitted not because it is ethically right, but because legislative and political institutions are thought to depend on the subordination of female to male, and of moral right and wrong to the making of expedient speeches and the passing of laws for what Plato would later call the 'advantage of the stronger', rather than justice in any ethical sense. The play carefully sidesteps the question of how daughters like Iphigenia will in future be protected from their fathers, or mothers like Clytemnestra from their sons.

Aeschylus, like all classical Greek poets, does not rhyme; his plays, like those of Sophocles and Euripides, are composed in a mix of metres, with relatively simple iambics for much of the dialogue, and complex metrical patterns for the choral passages, which were sung. In English translation, rhyming or other markedly poetic features can help hint at the difference between the dialogue and the choral passages. Aeschylus's language is much more difficult than that of Euripides, whose verse is often relatively conversational. Aeschylus's characters tend to speak in elaborate metaphors and peculiar, unidiomatic turns of phrase, many of which must have been lost on audience members sitting up high in the back rows of the theatre. Translators can simply ignore this altogether and render Aeschylus in prose, or they can try to replicate his dense riddling phrasing and complex metres, but there is a serious risk of substituting crabbed obscurity for an enigmatic richness of expression. Robert Browning's 1877 version of *Agamemnon* is arguably more difficult to understand than the Greek:

> Not gently-grieving, not just doling out
> The drops of expiation – no, nor tears distilled –
> Shall he we know of bring the hard about
> To soft – that intense ire
> At those mock rites unsanctified by fire.

The unidiomatic word order ('he we know of bring'), the peculiar syntax, including the abstract use of odd participles ('gently-grieving') and adjectives turned into nouns, and the dense mixed metaphors result in a weird poetic discourse, neither Greek nor entirely English. Aeschylus's sentence uses repeated negatives and emphatic half-rhymes to emphasise that nothing can remove the stain of child murder. But it does not include an equivalent to the weird 'he we know of' or the abstract nouns ('the hard' and 'the soft'), and it builds to a strong final main verb. Aeschylus is a difficult poet, and his work relies heavily on complex patterns of sound and imagery; but he is not quite as difficult as he sometimes seems in translation.

As we've seen, the dominant approach in anglophone translations of metrically regular classical verse, including drama, was to use stacked prose (or 'free verse'). In this mode there is a widely read unmetrical version of the *Oresteia* by Richmond Lattimore (1953), lightly revised by Mark Griffith and Glenn Most (2013). Lattimore turns Aeschylus's urgent, elaborately wrought Greek verse into peculiar English, which certainly does not scan and is not in any obvious sense poetic. For instance, a not very complicated line in which Athena declares her love for Athens becomes: 'So love I best of all / the unblighted generation of these upright men.' There is also an unmetrical, looser, more melodramatic version by Robert Fagles (1975), which tends, characteristically, to substitute English idioms and clichés for the original phrases, resulting in an Aeschylus who is much easier – possibly too easy – to read: 'Do we have to go on raking up old wounds? / Goodbye to all that.' Other unmetrical versions include a translation for the stage by Peter Meineck (1998) and many more free verse or prose versions (by Christopher Collard, Hugh Lloyd-Jones, Peter Burian, E. D. A. Morshead and others). Sarah Ruden's *Oresteia* (2016) demonstrated that the careful use of English metre without rhyme could be used to render Aeschylus in a poetic style that is difficult where appropriate without becoming unintelligible. Her translation of the sentence I quoted from Browning's version reads:

> Whatever's burned and poured and wept on altars
> won't coax away the anger tightly fastened
> to gifts no fire should touch.

Ruden matches the riddling strangeness of Aeschylus's language but makes the puzzle more or less possible to solve.

David Mulroy and Oliver Taplin adopt, at first glance, fairly similar approaches to Ruden and to each other: both use not only metre but also, for the lyrical choral passages, rhyme, to re-create something like the formal poetic effects of Aeschylus's elaborate verse style. I hope these translations are symptomatic of a trend in classical verse translations towards using more of the rich resources of anglophone poetics. Mulroy's handling of metre and rhyme is technically proficient: his lines scan, his rhymes rhyme, and he manages to combine these accomplishments with a rendering of the Greek that is reasonably accurate and fairly easy to understand. But his English is fussy, archaising and stiff. Here, again, is the triumphant Clytemnestra:

> I uttered many useful words before,
> which I won't blush at contradicting now.

'Blush at' makes the queen sound weirdly prudish. Ruden's rendering, also in regular iambic pentameter to honour the iambic trimeter of the original, is far more direct, and appropriately aggressive:

> Though all I said before was right for then,
> I'm not ashamed to state the opposite.

Taplin uses an iambic rhythm for the dialogue but in lines of uneven length. At first I found the variable line-lengths distracting, but the form grew on me; the admission of some longer lines allows him the flexibility to create vivid, plausible phrasing:

> I offer no apology for saying things that contradict
> what I have said before to suit the moment.

This is in certain ways further from the Greek than Ruden's version; Aeschylus has Clytemnestra say she 'won't be ashamed' (*ouk epaischunthēsomai*), not that she won't apologise, and she presents her current words as not only contradictory but 'opposite' (*t'anantia*) to what came before. But the swagger of Taplin's Clytemnestra is beautifully observed.

His use of alliteration and half-rhyme is particularly effective, and the dense mixed metaphors are often wonderfully well done. In the great first ode of *Agamemnon*, for example, I loved the image of eagles as 'terriers with wings' (although the dog breed is not specified in the Greek). Taplin tends to clarify and sometimes simplify Aeschylus's phrasing: the passage I quoted earlier from both Browning and Ruden, for instance, is stripped of some of its strange imagery, and the result is perhaps a little too easy, too quick:

> No amount of sacrificing
> can placate relentless anger.

But even if Taplin loses some of the original's linguistic complexity, he has created an English version full of sonic and metaphorical wealth, as when the Chorus sings of an obscure fate that should be spoken, but is not:

> it lurks in dark instead,
> and murmurs in its pain,
> and can't unwind the thread –
> meanwhile, my heart's aflame.

The rhyme and half-rhyme, here and elsewhere, create a sense of an ornately poetic and claustrophobic dramatic world.

Comparing Mulroy's version with the infinitely stronger work of Ruden and Taplin is a reminder of how hard it is to produce a good literary translation. This is certainly true of translations of ancient Greek and Roman texts, but it is also true of literary translation in general. Most readers of foreign languages are not translators; most writers are not translators. Translators have to read and write at the same time, as if always playing multiple instruments in a one-person band – and most one-person bands do not sound good. There are all too many moments when the choices in the weaker translations of Aeschylus are reminiscent of A. E. Housman's brilliant comic parody, 'Fragment of a Greek Tragedy'. Mulroy's Agamemnon, preparing to get his shoes taken off, calls: 'Undo / my shoes, the servile mats beneath my feet.' Attempts at more colloquial language fall flat: 'Bull's eye! The latter'; 'they're a violent lot'. The consistent thoughtlessness about linguistic register includes obliviousness about exclusive language and contemporary usage: Mulroy regularly uses 'man' and 'mankind' when the Greek refers to all, not half, of the human race. Cassandra makes a final heartbreaking expression of pity, not only for her own imminent murder, but for all mortal circumstances: *broteia pragmata*. Mulroy renders this 'Alas for men's affairs!' Taplin, far more effectively, has 'This is the way it is for humans.'

Taplin's is probably the best contemporary English rendition of the *Oresteia* in its evocation of Aeschylus's poetic range, dramatic power and moving awareness of pain, grief, confusion and rage. His rhythmical, alliterative, sometimes rhyming but often very direct language conveys real emotional power. I felt goosebumps at Cassandra's exchange with the Chorus, as she faces her death open-eyed: 'This is the day, today. To run away would gain me nothing.' Taplin recreates the incantatory music of Cassandra's prophecies,

Electra's laments and the Furies' enraged prayers. His language is rich in Aeschylean imagery and sound patterning without becoming impenetrable: 'We saw / the plain of the Aegean waters blossoming / with corpses of Greek men and debris of their ships.' The metaphorical images – dead bodies in the water resemble water-flowers, and these young men were also the 'flower' of Greece – are clear but not ponderous, conveying the horror of the large-scale loss of life.

Who belongs – in a family, a community, a city or a country? Can cycles of revenge and anger ever end? With the rise of autocratic populism and anti-immigrant sentiment around the world – ancient ideas in new forms – there is a renewed urgency to the themes raised by the *Oresteia*: exclusion and inclusion, tyranny, power, rage, justice, reparations, the proper function of democracy and the rule of law. As we turn our attention to the angry voices of those who feel themselves marginalised in modern life, it is worth turning back, with curious and critical eyes, to Aeschylus's great dramatic meditation on the politics of exclusion and on the exclusions entailed by politics itself, as well as the connections and gaps between justice and revenge. Perhaps, after all this time, we can begin to hear what the gagged, murdered Iphigenia might have wanted to say.

ANCIENT WORLDS: EDITH HAMILTON AND THE POPULARISATION OF THE CLASSICS

Social exclusion is an essential theme in ancient Greek tragedy and epic. It is also a central element in the formation of the modern discipline of 'classical studies', a field that has long been associated with gatekeeping. The mastery of Latin and ancient Greek – or, at least, knowing enough to trot out a well-worn tag from Horace and prompt knowing chuckles over the brandy – has often provided a useful qualification for passing as a gentleman and keeping out the plebs (Latin for 'common people') or hoi polloi (ancient Greek for 'the many'). It is understandable that George Eliot's Maggie Tulliver eagerly whizzes through the Latin textbooks neglected by her idle brother Tom, or that Thomas Hardy's Jude, hoping in vain to escape the obscurity of provincial poverty, slogs through his Greek dictionary until late into the night. For these fictional characters, like many of their real-life equivalents, ancient languages and literature provided the most visible bar against entry into a 'higher' social class.

Even in the twentieth and twenty-first centuries, the subject has maintained a close association with systems of exclusion based on income, education, race and gender. In the United Kingdom, its cultural capital remains high enough that Boris Johnson – an incompetent drunkard whose social privilege had enabled him to attend Eton and my own undergraduate alma mater, Balliol College, Oxford – managed to hold the highest political office in the land for an astonishingly long period of time, and even maintain the illusion of being an intellectual partly on the basis of his ability to parrot a few garbled lines of Homeric Greek. No other party trick could have served him as well. Thanks to centuries of culturally ingrained snobbery, even a passing acquaintance with these languages is still often considered a sign of extraordinary intelligence – as if it were really any harder to learn ancient Greek than it is to learn plumbing, Arabic or mechanical engineering.

Over the past century, there have been numerous attempts to make the supposed treasures of Greek and Roman antiquity accessible to those once excluded from its riches. In the early twentieth century, translations of ancient texts became more widely available, ranging from Gilbert Murray's wonderfully ornate and virtuosic renditions of Euripides to Hilda Doolittle's much starker modernist free verse. After the First World War, an ever-larger number of colleges and universities in the United States began to offer classes on ancient texts studied in translation, with no expectation that students would be able to read even a little of the originals. The study of ancient literature and history was often considered a prerequisite for understanding contemporary issues in Europe and the United States between the wars – regions that were then, as now, often lumped together under the term 'the West'. The Columbia Core, the first such course in the United States, was developed in 1919 with the explicit goal of showing students the 'unique features of the Western world', a world that apparently had begun in ancient Greece and that had now reached its apex in the American present.

The goal of connecting US citizens to a long, largely fabricated notion of 'Western civilisation' seemed increasingly urgent in the aftermath of a war that had torn the nations of Europe apart. The fantasy of a common 'Western' heritage shared by white Europeans and North Americans appeared as a prophylactic against future wars, at least between those who could qualify as 'Westerners'. But it also did something else. By excluding ancient texts and cultural artefacts from the rest of the world, these new courses suggested that premodern 'civilisation' was the exclusive property of the 'West' – enabling a mythical, quasi-historical justification for the West's dominion over the rest of the globe. Whether it was Black, Asian and Native American people in the United States, or the millions still living under imperial and colonial rule in Asia and Africa, the 'Western civilisation' framework implied that these histories were less valuable, and less ancient, than those of their colonisers.

By the 1920s, a sizeable market for popular classics books and translations had emerged. A new publishing firm, W. W. Norton, decided to seize on it and signed up a recently retired Latin teacher and private school headmistress named Edith Hamilton to translate a trio of Greek tragedies and write two surveys of ancient literature, *The Greek Way* and *The Roman Way*. Published in quick succession in the 1930s, these volumes were an immediate success. Along with *Mythology*, her retelling of the Graeco-Roman legends, the books made Hamilton a household name. *Mythology* has never been out of print since then and has remained an extraordinary commercial success, enriching her heirs and publishers to this day. Probably no other single person has had such an impact in shaping popular perceptions of classical literature and mythology in the United States.

How did a retired Latin schoolteacher (Hamilton was sixty-two when *The Greek Way* was published), with few scholarly credentials, come to be one of the most influential 'classicists' of the twentieth century? The answer lies both with Hamilton's own specific gifts as a writer and populariser of ancient literature, and with the particular cultural moment in which she lived. She was born in 1867, the eldest in a family of four daughters and one son, the youngest, who was always known as Quintus – a mild joke (*quintus* is the Latin for 'fifth') that hints at the family's educational aspirations. She grew up on her father's homestead in Fort Wayne, Indiana. Montgomery Hamilton was a heavy drinker who proved unsuccessful in running his family's business, but he was eager to educate his children, including the daughters. All were homeschooled, and Edith began learning Latin and ancient Greek from her father as a child. At sixteen, she was sent to a finishing school in Connecticut. She spent another few years at home in

Indiana, waiting for her family to rustle up the money for college and filling in the gaps in her mathematical and linguistic preparation. She eventually passed the entrance exams at the recently founded Bryn Mawr College, performing well enough to acquire a bachelor's and then a master's degree, with a focus on the Latin of Seneca, in just over three years.

After graduation, Hamilton was appointed as headmistress of the newly established Bryn Mawr School for Girls in Baltimore. She accepted the job reluctantly, but nonetheless remained for almost thirty years, from 1896 to 1922. Her success as a headmistress speaks to her enormous talents as a visionary leader, administrator and networker. Hamilton was able to fuse her passion for educating girls in Greek and Latin with ideas of 'individual self-realization' borrowed from John Dewey, whom she met in 1898. Dewey, a philosopher, psychologist and educational reformer, argued that teachers should train the democratic citizens of the future, by inspiring students to gain the full use of their own capabilities. The most important goal was not to impart knowledge or even skills in the ignorant youth, but to generate 'a higher standard of intelligence in the community' (to quote his 'The Teacher and the Public').

Hamilton built a reputation for classes that were civically as well as academically improving, and the wealthy families of Baltimore bought what Hamilton was selling – her school became a major economic and social success. On one level, it opened the gates of classical learning to a social group – wealthy white girls – who had previously been shut out of the joys of Greek and Latin; but on another level, the social barriers of wealth and race were very much reinforced. The students were all white, and Jewish girls were not made welcome at the school, although Hamilton herself did not object to hiring Jewish teachers.

Hamilton's later work as a translator and a populariser of ancient literature constantly drew on her experiences in the classroom. But she began this work only after she had retired from the school and had begun a new relationship with a much younger woman, Doris Reid (Hamilton's romantic relationships were exclusively with women). Together with their adopted son, Hamilton's nephew, they moved from Baltimore to New York City, where new opportunities awaited. Hamilton dated the start of her writing career to a friendship with Edith J. R. Isaacs, a neighbour and friend who edited *Theatre Arts Monthly* and encouraged her to write the essays that became *The Greek Way*. But many others soon came knocking at Hamilton's door, including Elling Aannestad, an editorial assistant at W. W. Norton, the publisher that would acquire *The Greek Way*, *The Roman Way*, and Hamilton's translations of Aeschylus's *Agamemnon*, the perhaps-Aeschylean *Prometheus Bound*, and Euripides' *Trojan Women*. The choice of plays reflects Hamilton's conventional, already old-fashioned perception of Greek tragedy as a genre focused on noble suffering: Greek tragedies with happy endings and little wailing – such as Euripides' *Helen* or *Ion* – were of less interest to her. The Norton books soon caught the attention of other publishers, and at the prompting of C. Raymond Everitt, an editor at Little, Brown, Hamilton began working on *Mythology*, which would be her greatest commercial triumph.

Hamilton's popular, often wildly inaccurate accounts of the ancient world were out of step with the analyses of scholars in her own time, let alone with contemporary perspectives. Her idealised vision of a liberated, enlightened ancient Greece – a culture that she presents, with horrifying racial prejudice, as fundamentally superior to other, benightedly primitive ancient cultures, such as Egypt – is starkly at odds with the view put forth in E. R. Dodds's *The Greeks and the Irrational* (1951). Dodds's book might seem to have put paid to such false notions forever, in its clear-eyed account of the centrality of irrational, magical, religious and superstitious elements in ancient Greek culture, and its insistence that the Greeks were not more civilised or more keen on freedom than any other group of people, ancient or modern. And yet, thanks in large part to Hamilton, these bogus ideas persist within popular understanding of antiquity. Homeric scholarship in the early twentieth century had also made enormous progress in understanding how Greek oral poetics developed over many generations of folk tradition, and Hamilton's scholarly contemporaries understood that some ancient poetry was a collaborative endeavour that evolved over time and was, crucially, not the work of a single author. Hamilton's still-canonical account of Greek myth and Homeric poetry entirely lacks these nuances, relying on the idea that ancient 'great books' were always created by individual 'great men' – concepts that lurk in current popular perceptions of antiquity.

Perhaps unsurprisingly, Hamilton expressed very little interest in the civil rights movements of her time. She and Reid moved to Washington, D.C. in 1943, and their social circle leaned increasingly to the right. Reid became active in conservative politics, adopting positions that might now be seen as libertarian: she favoured American isolationism and was obsessively anti-communist. Of course, none of these views are explicitly stated in Hamilton's books, but they can be glimpsed in her account of ancient Greece as a magical land of democratic liberty, free from the taint of tyranny that, according to Hamilton, afflicted other ancient and modern societies.

Despite her German birth, Hamilton was very American. I grew up in the UK and had barely heard of her until a few years ago. Yet in the US, Hamilton's work has played an enormous role in making classical studies popular and accessible. Her books, especially *Mythology*, retain their hold on the American reading public for several reasons. One is their fluent, vivid and vigorous style, reminiscent of the most effective and inspirational kind of old-fashioned high-school Latin teacher. The prose is very lightly archaic and vaguely biblical, which helps to establish the author's claim to an authoritative knowledge of the world of antiquity and ancient legends: 'But Jason withstood the fearful creatures as a great rock in the sea withstands the waves.' It is truly gripping stuff, especially good for reading out loud. Hamilton's years of storytelling in the classroom to her Baltimore pupils paid many dividends. Purely as a stylist, Hamilton deserves her status in the bestseller ranks.

Another reason for Hamilton's grip on the American reading public is that she remakes ancient Greece in the image of an idealised United States – a world of glorious individualism and democratic freedom for all (or at least for everyone supposed to matter). She paints a largely imaginary portrait of ancient Greece as the birthplace of 'individualism', 'democracy' and 'the West' – in other words, as the precursor to a privileged white person's idealised notion of America. Hamilton hardly ever provides any caveats to the notions of ancient Greek 'freedom' and 'democracy' (such as the fact that the vast majority of the population of ancient Athens was disenfranchised, and a great many people were enslaved). She relies heavily on vague, more or less unprovable claims about 'spirit': 'To rejoice in life, to find the world beautiful and delightful to live in', she writes in one of many such passages, 'was a mark of the Greek spirit which distinguished it from all that had gone before.' Hamilton created an image of ancient Greece that was alien enough to sound romantic, but also familiar to a readership of white Americans eager to imagine themselves as the proud inhabitants of a land of freedom and superiority.

Moreover, in much of her writing, Hamilton maintains a constant aura of authority on the page, not least by interweaving her summaries and discussions with little snippets of ancient texts, translated in a very loose, evocative style and with no source ever provided. The reader is encouraged to take their accuracy as a matter of faith, not research. The most famous such snippet, from Aeschylus's *Agamemnon*, was quoted by Senator Robert F. Kennedy, a great admirer of Hamilton, after the assassination of Martin Luther King Jr: 'In our sleep, pain which cannot forget falls drop by drop upon the heart until, in our own despair, against our will, comes wisdom through the awful grace of God.' Kennedy, who also claimed Aeschylus as his favourite poet, was misquoting Hamilton from memory – and Hamilton's translation was itself both slapdash and domesticising, rendering the plural 'gods' as the appropriately American 'God'. Hamilton's version of ancient Greece conveys an aura of power, strangeness and grandeur from her starkly magniloquent prose – while also providing a highly Americanised, vaguely Christianised vision of what these texts may have to say. The ancient Greece of Hamilton's writing is never fundamentally challenging to a modern white American Christian world view. Her modernising distortions, falsehoods and projections of the present onto the past are mostly masked by her fine rhetoric. Her books are therefore ideally suited for the many twenty-first-century schools, teachers and homeschooling parents in search of wholesome, 'traditional' fare for their curricula.

The casual, often quite explicit racism of Hamilton's account of Greece and 'the West' may also play a part in her continuing appeal. At the start of *The Greek Way*, Hamilton insisted on the superiority of the (Western, implicitly white) Greeks over the 'ignorant', 'subjugated', and 'wretched' peoples of 'the East'. Later, without any particular knowledge of ancient Egyptian or Asian civilisations (beyond a couple of fun vacations to these exotic locales), Hamilton blithely dismissed them as containing 'human beings ... who are only partially developed', lacking the complete unity of 'mind and spirit' that was present only in ancient Greece, until its reappearance, at last, in America. The reissued version of *Mythology* still includes Hamilton's preamble claiming that Greek myth, being characterised by enlightenment, is 'worlds apart' from the 'primeval slime' represented by 'New Guinea today' and 'the Egyptians'. Even reviewers at the time of her first book's publication (such as Percy Hutchison in *The New York Times*) observed that Hamilton's stark distinction between 'East' and 'West' was, historically, complete nonsense.

There is one last possible reason for Hamilton's continuing commercial success: the lack of an obvious heir. D'Aulaires' *Greek Myths* is a picture book designed for significantly younger readers. There have been many more recent retellings of Greek and Roman myths for adult and young adult readers, including Stephen Fry's *Mythos*, *Heroes*, *Troy* and *Odyssey*, and Sarah Iles Johnston's fine *Gods and Mortals*. But neither writes with the resonant (albeit often unearned) panache and authority of Hamilton. It is hard to think of a contemporary writer who fills anything like the cultural position she enjoyed in the mid-twentieth century. Fry's comic, self-ironising pomposity of tone recalls the school-teacherly register of Hamilton's prose, but in an ironized, distant mode, and largely to Fry's credit, he does not pretend to offer the grand ideological vision of *Mythology*. Similarly, Natalie Haynes' various retellings of Greek and Roman myth and literature package them into easily recognisable modern tropes – girl power, second-wave feminism, stand-up comedy. These retellings do not suggest, as Hamilton so often does, that an engagement with antiquity could change your soul, and maybe the world. In the UK, the most famous contemporary classicist is Mary Beard, who is different from Hamilton in that she had a scholarly career as an academic ancient historian. She is far less interested than Hamilton was in poetics or myth, but Beard, like Hamilton, is a public figure who has used her training in a small subfield of ancient studies to acquire a soapbox as an oracular authority on all things everywhere, from Brexit to the global history of culture and the internet. Each of these figures – Fry, Haynes and Beard – are like Hamilton in that they have gained popular success by fusing a schtick about classics with something much more nebulous and hard to achieve: a popular persona.

In our day, as in Hamilton's, many of the most successful popularisations of the classics have been created by those who are not themselves classicists. This even applies to many of the bestselling translators of ancient Greek and Roman literature: Robert Fagles trained in English literature, E. V. Rieu was a publisher, Robert Fitzgerald a journalist. It is an even more notable pattern for the most prominent retellings of ancient stories and myths. Stephen Fry, for instance, is a comic actor with no training in classics but great rhetorical gifts, whose plummy, humorous retellings of ancient myths have proved extraordinarily popular, especially in his native Britain. Similarly, Tom Holland has gained enormous success with historical non-fiction and historical novels set in the ancient world, despite no training in the field – again, especially in his native UK.

Some of the most memorable contemporary creative work inspired by ancient literature uses the strangeness of antiquity to reinvigorate the current literary landscape. Alice Oswald's extraordinary *Memorial* – an 'excavation' of the *Iliad* through its deaths – points to new possibilities for imagery and the representation of loss in contemporary poetics, through a deep engagement with Homer. Madeline Miller's heartbreaking novella, *Song of Achilles* (2011), helped to make the representation of queer love stories more mainstream, through her retelling of the central relationship of the *Iliad* as a doomed romance. Oswald has a BA in classics from Oxford, and Miller an MA in classics from Brown. Creative people who have engaged deeply with the ancient languages and cultures may have the best chance of making the strangeness of ancient literature viscerally accessible to a contemporary reader.

Most twenty-first-century culture based on ancient Greek myth or literature tends to recast ancient stories and characters in the framework of modern, twenty-first-century concerns. Anne Carson's cult classic, *Autobiography of Red*, is an odd book in several ways, combining essayistic riffs on the ancient poet Stesichorus, and snippets of translation, with a set of characters (Heracles, Geryon) who are transferred from ancient Greek poetry to contemporary Canada. But this 'novel in verse' is neither strange nor ancient in its central themes of abuse and unhappy romance – topics that are not central in any surviving archaic Greek literature. Numerous less weird modern novelisations – the novels of Jennifer Saint, Miller's *Circe*, Pat Barker's *The Silence of the*

Girls and *Women of Troy*, Natalie Haynes' *Stone Blind* and *A Thousand Ships*, and many, many more – rework Greek myths as stories of female oppression and empowerment, with varying degrees of literary ambition and literary success. Rick Riordan's childrens' series, the Percy Jackson books, borrow characters from ancient Greek mythology, but use antiquity mainly as backdrop for an entirely contemporary set of narrative themes, about how courageous American teenagers can rid the world of feminised, racially othered monsters, through pluck and team-work. Similarly, familiar modern ideas of idealised machismo and superhero saviours shape many contemporary adaptations of ancient literature and myth for the screen, such as Wolfgang Petersen's *Troy* and the even more cartoonishly toxic *300*.

Armchair classicists often lay claim to a radically simplified and distorted version of the ancient world, shaped by modern ideological projections and constructions of 'tradition' that map suspiciously well onto contemporary right-wing values and contemporary Catholic or evangelical beliefs. Gatekeeping around the classics, like gate-opening, is most often performed by those who are not classicists – from the endless opinion pieces from non-classicists telling us how to do our jobs or pontificating about the imminent end of the discipline, to the trolls who pounce on a Homerist who makes the basic error of being female in public. By contrast, actual scholars of ancient literature often like the idea of making the discipline more inclusive, without necessarily knowing how.

What, then, can be done by those of us within the

palace of classics who hope, like Princess Anna in *Frozen*, to open up the gates? We could do worse than take notes from Hamilton, despite her woolly thinking, prejudices, distortions and errors. She engaged the reading public in something a little bit like the study of ancient Greece, not by actual knowledge or credentials, but by the unfeigned enthusiasm and devotion with which she told and retold the story of her love for her own imagined, idealised version of antiquity. Her enduring influence demonstrates the hunger of educators, students and the public for accessible, engaging accounts of ancient literature – while also reminding us that it is difficult to teach and to learn new things.

Original scholarship, in classical studies as in other fields, requires deep, wide, responsible research and insightful, creative thinking. It need not require the scholar to be a particularly good writer – and indeed, many of the finest scholars are somewhere between mediocre and abysmal when it comes to prose style. But successful public scholarship requires, above all, an engaging literary style. Hamilton's work may be lazy and derivative in its content, but it is brilliantly resonant and memorable in its distinctive voice on the page – and this is no easy feat. Public perceptions of ancient literature, as of other areas within the humanities, are very often outdated, domesticated and simplified, thanks in no small part to Hamilton, as well as Fry, Haynes and others. This, in turn, contributes to false perceptions that ancient literature is only an older view on the same world. Readers could be forgiven for thinking there's nothing new to learn about the ancient world. If scholars want any of these things to change, we need to begin training ourselves and our students not only how to conduct careful, thorough, generative research, but also how to engage with the public beyond the academy. We must show members of the intelligent reading public the respect they deserve, by offering nuanced, clear, interesting analyses of antiquity in all its glorious, alien complexity. To do that, above all, we need to learn how to write.

TRANSLATING THE *ODYSSEY*

Mistakes are possible in translation, as every language instructor knows. But there is never a single 'correct' translation of a specific word, phrase, sentence or passage. There are a wide variety of responsible ways to create an equivalent, just as there are many ways to play a single score of music, many ways to paint the same landscape, and many ways to direct a play or deliver a speech.

This point applies to translation in general, not only literary translation, and not only translation from ancient languages. The text on a shampoo bottle or a menu or a street sign can, like an ancient epic poem, be translated several different ways. Idiomatic metaphors, syntax and socio-linguistic connotations are rarely the same across languages. But this general fact can be hard to absorb in the abstract, especially for people who are not themselves practising translators. A simple way to glimpse the range of possible approaches to translation, and to get a first taste of how approaches to translation have changed over time, is to look at several different retranslations of the same passage.

This essay is inspired by a set of threads I wrote on what was then Twitter, in the wake of the publication of my translation of the *Odyssey* in 2017, in which I used close reading to invite readers to a more precise awareness of what's at stake in the variety of Homeric translations into English. I have heard from many teachers who have used these threads in their classroom and found it useful to generate student discussion. So I provide here a new version of this exercise, to provide a more explicit account of this book's central ideas about the pleasures and perils of translation. A close examination of the numerous English translations of Homer reminds us how very difficult it is to recreate something like the meanings, effects, sounds and rhythms of ancient poetry in English – a language that did not exist in ancient times. And yet the enormous variation between Homeric translations also shows the vast range of ways we can reimagine antiquity, and illuminate the surprising gaps and connections between the ancient world and our own.

I have prioritised the translations that are most commonly read and cited in the contemporary anglophone world, and those that most clearly represent distinct approaches to the retranslation of the *Odyssey*. These priorities are slightly in tension with one another: several of these translations are quite similar in approach – unsurprisingly, since humans are mimetic animals. It is also worth looking at a couple of important pre-twentieth-century translations, to appreciate how shifts in our own culture have shaped approaches to translation more broadly. The earliest are the marvellous translations into rhyming fourteeners (for the *Iliad*) and rhyming pentameter couplets (for the *Odyssey*) by the great

Elizabethan/Jacobean poet of revenge tragedies, George Chapman. Chapman was the first person to publish complete translations of these epics into English (1616, with instalments appearing earlier). His *Seven Books of the Iliades* was a source for Shakespeare's *Troilus and Cressida*. I also discuss the sublime rhyming couplet translation by the eighteenth-century poet Alexander Pope. By modern standards of translation, both Chapman and Pope often seem more like 'imitations' than translations – a fact that itself illustrates a historical shift in literary translation practices.

I also look at more recent examples, including the peculiar prose translation by the satirical Victorian novelist Samuel Butler (1900). This version is odd in interesting ways, and is still fairly widely read, perhaps largely because it is out of copyright and therefore available for free online – and maybe also because of the misperception that prose is easier to read than verse. Another, very different in approach and style, is the verse translation by Robert Fitzgerald (1961), which uses a largely iambic rhythm and is notable for its artful use of literary allusions and poeticisms. From the same era and also from the US, Richmond Lattimore's 1965 translation uses long, unmetrical lines (no iambs or dactyls are audible here), and an unidiomatic, archaising style. Lattimore is often touted as the most 'literal' translator (although, as we've seen, the reputation for extraordinary fidelity is not fully deserved). Another important example of the 'literal' style is the prose translation published by the Loeb Classical Library in archaising prose by A. T. Murray, lightly revised by George Dimock in 1995. I also look at what was by some distance the bestselling American version for a good twenty years, Robert Fagles' lively, often melodramatic version in unmetrical free verse (1995). Stanley Lombardo's snappy, slangy translation in very chatty free verse (2000) reads sometimes like a stripped-down adaptation of Fagles; it is still quite popular with instructors hoping to coach reluctant readers through the *Odyssey* in a short time. I hope this sampling will provide at least a glimpse of the rich array of choices facing the translator.

My primary goal in looking closely at a few translations side by side is to show readers who cannot access the Greek the multifarious ways of responding responsibly to the same original. Not all of these translators' choices are equally valid. I myself spend many hours of every day wrestling with alternative possibilities in my own translations in progress, in an eternal quest to find a better solution – a more truthful evocation of a poetic experience that might parallel that of the original. I go through innumerable drafts, and I am always aware that my 'final' drafts include numerous compromises: the goal, for me and for all of us, is not the perfect translation, but a translation that is, for now, better than anything else I could come up with.

But what counts as 'better' depends, as this exercise demonstrates, on the translator's priorities. Recreating the traditional metre of the original is a priority for some, and not at all for others. Some try for an equivalent emotional effect; some strive for an equivalent register; some for similar word order or similar syntax. It is often impossible to achieve all these things in the same translation. One of these approaches is not 'right' while the others are 'wrong': rather, each reflects a different way to present the original poetic style in a new linguistic and literary context.

When you look at these translations alongside each other, it soon becomes clear that translators have tried numerous different styles of language to make their English match the Greek. For poets in the eras of Chapman or Pope, it would have been unthinkable to translate Homer into prose (let alone free verse, which of course did not yet exist). But for many in the twentieth and twenty-first centuries, variations on more or less grandiloquent prose, or prose laid out as verse, have been viewed not only as the most authentic, but also as the most 'poetic' ways of approaching the translation of the Homeric poems. The English language has changed since the time of Pope or even Butler, but, more importantly, readers' perceptions of what counts as 'poetic' have changed. Readers with no ear for metre are far more common than they once were. Moreover, the general perception of Homeric poems is quite different in the twenty-first century. *The Odyssey* is now ultra-canonical, and often viewed as a wellspring of 'Western civilisation', whatever that may be, whereas in the time of Pope, when the *Aeneid* was far more central to the canon.

All translators know that any word, phrase, sentence or passage in one language can be rendered into another language in a thousand forms. The choices are not infinite, but they are always multiple. The ancient Greek word *anēr* cannot mean 'woman', 'bunny rabbit', or 'buttered toast'. But it can mean either 'man' or 'husband' – and the choice might matter. Also, the connotations of both 'man' and 'husband' in English are not the same as those of the ancient Greek word, because our assumptions about gender and marriage are not the same – an insuperable but ever-present problem, created by the intertwining of language with its social contexts. The choices are all the more difficult because language is not simply a list of nouns: syntax and word order vary across languages. Ancient Greek, like other highly inflected languages, can vary word order much more than English can, so it is very difficult for a translator to recreate the word order or syntax of the original without creating a text that is significantly less idiomatic and less fluent. A translator of poetry may also want to take account of sound, rhythm, metre, alliteration, assonance, voice, perspective, mood, register, emotional effect, pacing, imagery, idiom, and a dozen other essential qualities of the original – or they may choose to ignore these things, in favour of other kinds of truth. How can we replicate all of the original text's qualities and effects, using none of the same words? There is no obvious solution. And yet we try.

My first example is the first two lines of Book 5 of the *Odyssey*.

> Ἠὼς δ' ἐκ λεχέων παρ' ἀγαυοῦ Τιθωνοῖο ὤρνυθ',
> ἵν' ἀθανάτοισι φόως φέροι ἠδὲ βροτοῖσιν.

The lines are an interesting variation on the more usual 'rosy-fingered Dawn' (*rhododaktulos Ēōs*). At the start of

Book 5, we meet Odysseus trapped on the island of the goddess Calypso, whose name suggests 'hiding'. He spends his days weeping by the shore, longing for home, and his nights with the goddess, with whom he has spent seven years. The text leads us to believe that Odysseus's feelings have changed, and that he may at some earlier time have enjoyed his time with this mysterious goddess: he longs for a homecoming now, 'because the goddess no longer brought him joy' (ἐπεὶ οὐκέτι ἥνδανε νύμφη). And yet he cannot escape: this deity detains him on her island 'by necessity'. In response to Odysseus's suffering, his eternally asexual patron goddess, Athena, has persuaded her father, Zeus, that they must send the messenger god, Hermes, to tell Calypso that she has to let her mortal consort go home to his mortal wife – back to the sphere in which he can achieve glory and an eternal name, which would be impossible if he were to accept Calypso's offer to make him immortal and ageless, as her eternal lover.

The opening lines of the book remind us that Calypso is not the only goddess to have taken up with a mortal man. Dawn abducted Tithonus, a Trojan prince, and asked Zeus to make him immortal – but she failed to ask that he also be ageless, so he became shrivelled and weak, despite being unable to die. In later versions of the myth, he was transformed into a cicada. The parallel between Dawn and Calypso reminds us of the dangers that face a mortal man bedded by a goddess; for all her promises, divine Calypso threatens Odysseus's power and autonomy, unless he can escape from her. Unlike Calypso, Dawn has managed to keep her lover in her bed forever – whereas Calypso will soon be pressured by Hermes into letting her man go.

With Homer's usual restraint, none of the implications of the parallel are directly spelled out. But they are hinted at. In the second line, Dawn brings light to two very different groups of beings: the 'deathless' and 'mortals', who are denoted by words that are not etymologically or sonically related: *athanatoisi* ... *brotoisin*. The groups are together in that they share the same bright early light; but they are separated in the line, just as Dawn separates herself from Tithonus, and Odysseus will soon separate himself from Calypso. A final important parallel between these two lines and what follows is that Dawn is, like Hermes, a messenger who travels a long distance to bring light and enlightenment to two different kinds of being – one immortal, and one not. None of this is easy for a translator to reproduce with the same verve as the original.

Here are those two lines in the first complete published English translation, in fine rhyming couplets by George Chapman:

> AURORA rose from high-born Tithon's bed,
> That men and Gods might be illustrated.

'Illustrate' was, in Chapman's time, used in the same sense as to 'illuminate' the mind. There is apparently no instance (according to the *Oxford English Dictionary*) of 'illustrate' meaning only 'to shed light on' before 1625, so when Chapman was writing these lines, the primary connotation is that Dawn is bringing not merely physical, literal light, but enlightenment. Chapman was a Christian Neo-Stoic, and his interest in reading the *Odyssey* as a story of spiritual and educational progress is legible even in these ostensibly quite simple lines.

Now here is the eighteenth-century version by an equally brilliant poet, Alexander Pope, who had his own, very different, concept of Enlightenment. His translation is also in rhyming couplets.

> The saffron morn, with early blushes spread,
> Now rose refulgent from Tithonus' bed

As is typical for his translation style, Pope adds several details that are not in the Greek, including the colour of 'morn' (she is not saffron or any other colour in the Greek), and the cute detail of the 'blushes'. This version of 'morn' seems to be doing the walk of shame – embarrassed to be getting up from her adulterous bed. The morals and norms of Pope's own time are clearly discernible in his translation. No archaic Greek goddess would feel the need to blush about being sexually active. It is also notable that both Pope and Chapman claim that the bed belongs to Tithonus. This is not suggested in the Greek, and would surely have been a surprising idea for an archaic Greek audience, given that the immortal goddess has chosen to share her abode, and her bed, with a kidnapped, powerless mortal. He could surely not be expected to bring his own furniture. But the mores of seventeenth- and eighteenth-century England have crept into the translations of this archaic Greek poem, such that the bed must belong to the male partner – no matter what nonsense it makes of the narrative.

In the early nineteenth century, the hymnodist, abolitionist and celebrated nature poet, William Cowper, created another version in unrhyming blank verse (1791).

> Aurora from beside her glorious mate
> Tithonus now arose, light to dispense
> Through earth and heav'n …

Cowper is noticeably loose, one could say inaccurate, in his domesticising rendition of the 'deathless gods … mortals': 'earth and heav'n' is not the same as 'those who die and those who live forever'. The translation depersonalises, and imports language more familiar from Cowper's hymns to his *Odyssey*. The marked prissiness of 'dispense' is an interesting choice, given that the Greek verb *pheroi* is an extremely common word for 'bring'. Using dispense gives an almost medicinal tone to the scene. Cowper suffered from bouts of extreme depression and suicidality. He was dependent on opium, and relied on the numerous 'opium dispensaries' (the term in current usage at his time of writing) that provided relief for those in need of the sedating poppy. Cowper may or may not have been consciously making the connection, but his rendition of this scene seems to hint that Aurora resembles those kind pharmacists: she is dispensing the good stuff both on earth and in heaven.

Here's Samuel Butler's prose translation from the turn of the twentieth century.

> And now, as Dawn rose from her couch beside Tithonus – harbinger of light alike to mortals and immortals …

The use of 'harbinger' strikes me as misleading: the Greek says that Dawn actually brings the light, not that she is the announcer of light that is being conveyed by some other means. I would also note that the addition of 'alike' and the very neat parallelism of 'mortals and immortals', with the 'mortals' put first, creates an effect quite different from the Greek, which uses words from two different linguistic roots, and separates them: Butler suggests that mortals and immortals are very much the same, at least in how they experience light – whereas an essential point in the first half of Book 5 is that mortals and immortals are not, and should not be, as close as all that. Butler also skips Tithonus's honorific epithet.

From the twentieth century, the Loeb Classical Library prose version, by A. T Murray and revised by George Dimock, reads as follows:

> Now Dawn arose from her couch from beside lordly Tithonus, to bear light to the immortals and to mortal men.

The Loeb, with its parallel printing of the original next to the translation, is often imagined to be the most 'literal', in the sense of being measurably more accurate than prettier versions could be. But this is debatable in general: if the original is noticeably beautiful, elegant and poetic, the translation should arguably reflect those qualities. In this pair of lines, there are several questionable choices. For instance, the translation adds 'her' to the 'couch' and adds 'men' to the mortals: the Greek does not say to whom the bed belongs, and does not suggest that light falls only on males. Clunky repetition ('from … from') is noticeable in the translation, where the original has elegant variation of prepositions (*ek … par*). The translation also introduces a great many archaisms, including 'couch' (for 'bed'), 'bear', 'arose', and 'lordly'. None of the words in the Homeric Greek are unusual in the context of the poem, and most of them were still in usage in later, classical (or Attic) Greek – so it seems unlikely that their effect was quite as fancy or distanced as the lexicon chosen here. One might also debate the choice to render metrical poetry in prose.

I've heard people express affection for the admirably peculiar prose translation by T. E. Lawrence (1932), so here it is:

> Dawn rose from her marriage-bed beside high-born Tithonus to bring her daylight to both gods and men.

Lawrence is the only translator of those I have looked at for this exercise who makes the coupled pair actually married – which the Greek certainly does not imply. Given the various rumours about Lawrence's sexual proclivities, it seems possible that he here works particularly hard to assure us that everything is above board and bourgeois in the world of the *Odyssey*. Lawrence also generously insists that both the bed and the light itself belong to Dawn (which is not said or implied in the Greek). The translation 'gods and men' removes the specific focus on mortality/immortality, which is the point of the binary in the Greek.

Here is the version by Robert Fitzgerald, from 1961:

> Dawn came up from the couch of her reclining,
> leaving her lord Tithonus' brilliant side
> with fresh light in her arms for gods and men.

Fitzgerald was a good poet, and he makes interesting use of rhythm in his translations; the second and third lines here are in regular iambic pentameter, while the first line has a more trochaic beat. Fitzgerald avoided regular metre deliberately, on the advice of Ezra Pound, and reflections of Pound's poetic sensibility can also be heard in Fitzgerald's use of allusive, often vaguely biblical, markedly 'literary' language. The original is, of course, all in regular traditional metre, and Fizgerald's poeticisms do not always map onto anything particular in the Greek. For instance, like the Loeb translators, he makes poor old Dawn sleep on the couch. If it were 1750, a couch would be a very different thing. And yet the Greek word *lechos* would probably not have felt noticeably archaic to a listener of Homer in the fifth century BCE, given that this is the same word used for 'bed' by Sophocles, Euripides and Aristophanes.

The 'brilliant side' is a strange and interesting addition;

a literal-minded reader might wonder if he is less brilliant when he flips over. Tithonus, doomed to eternal life without eternal youth, was turned into a cicada: Fitzgerald's translation perhaps suggests that he is shiny like a cicada (although none of that is suggested by the Greek). 'Reclining' and 'leaving' are also noticeable additions, which make Dawn a more leisurely, idle figure than she may seem from the Greek. The translation also makes Tithonus important not for his status in general (as per the Greek), but for his status over her – 'her' lord. It is tempting to speculate that the personal experiences of thrice-married Fitzgerald might have influenced his representations of such relationships in the *Odyssey*. My favourite additions in this translation are the 'arms' and the 'fresh', creating a lovely image of Dawn holding light as if it were a bouquet of newly gathered flowers – which could not possibly be got from the Greek, but is in itself quite charming.

Here is the unmetrical verse version of Richmond Lattimore, published in 1963, soon after Fitzgerald's:

> Now Dawn rose from her bed, where she lay by
>   haughty Tithonus,
> carrying light to the immortal gods and to
>   mortals …

Although they are from the same country and era, Lattimore and Fitzgerald are very different in their approach to Homeric translation, to poetics, and to the poem's sexual mores. 'Haughty' is a strangely judgemental choice for a word, *agauos*, that is generally used to suggest 'general commendation', 'usually applied to elite characters', to quote Richard Cunliffe's *A Lexicon of the Homeric Dialect* – a key resource for any translator of Homer. 'Haughty' is usually a negative term, unlike *agauos*; one might detect in the translation an implicit criticism of this man who has the chutzpah to carry on his illicit affair up there in the sky. Lattimore adds several details that are not strictly in the Greek: 'her' bed, 'where she lay', and 'now'. His syntax is also quite different from the Greek: Homer's Dawn gets up in order to bring light (a purpose clause, with a finite verb); Lattimore's Dawn is blessed with a present participle ('carrying'), such that she seems to be lumbered with the light even while she is still abed. In general, this translator has a great fondness for participles, and often uses them even when the Greek has finite verbs that create a far more energetic effect. All this is worth spelling out, because Lattimore is often represented and seen as a particularly faithful translator. In fact, we all interpret. We dance different ways along the tightrope, trying to balance all the different truths.

I pause here for a note on metre. People have frequently told me adamantly that Lattimore's Homeric translations are in dactylic hexameter, the metre of the original. This is false. I am not casting aspersions on an honoured and late-lamented colleague; Lattimore knew quite well that his lines were not hexameter, and he also made no claim to be writing 'poetry', whatever that may be. Lattimore's lines have a range of different types of feet, and there are frequently more or fewer than six main beats in the line. To take this little sample as a metrical test case: in the first line, we have spondee, dactyl, dactyl, trochee, dactyl, spondee; the next definitely has only five feet at most, and definitely has two iambs (dactyl, dactyl, iamb, iamb, pyrrhic, trochee – an oddly trailing effect). There is no sign of rhythm. This stacked prose has some dactyls sometimes, but many other rhythms too, as prose does. The model of using irregular, unmetrical but long, meandering, often idiomatic lines to translate the Homeric dactylic hexameter has proven extremely popular in the twenty-first century, with a great many other anglophone translators following more or less the Lattimore model: these include versions by Peter Green, Barry Powell, Antony Verity, Caroline Alexander (*Iliad* only) and Daniel Mendelsohn (*Odyssey* only).

Published to great acclaim in 1996, here is the free verse version by Robert Fagles:

> As Dawn rose up from bed by her lordly mate
>   Tithonus,
> bringing light to immortal gods and mortal men …

The Greek has no word equivalent to 'mate', and its insertion makes a difference; it suggests an almost animalistic pairing that sits slightly strangely beside the grand, vaguely archaic 'lordly'. The Greek does not label the relationship in any way; the listener is presumed to know how Dawn and Tithonus are connected. Like Lattimore and Fitzgerald, Fagles changes the purpose clause of the Greek to a participle ('bringing'); as a result, in all of these translations, Dawn's work of bringing light seems to happen without her conscious intent to carry it out. This is a significant change, because it reduces the connection between Dawn and Hermes, who are both travellers with a purpose. It is also interesting that Fagles, like several other translators, adds both 'gods' and 'men'. You might think that everyone, including women and goddesses, might share the experience of Dawn's light (and the Greek word *brotos* is used with a feminine article later in *Odyssey* book 5, line 334, to describe the White Goddess, Ino). Fagles eliminates the possibility that those blessed with light could be female. Perhaps he adds the nouns for sonic reasons: his rhythms are irregular but tending to iambic, and the addition of the nouns allows the line to resolve into a predominantly iambic sound.

Here is the free verse version by Stanley Lombardo (2000).

> Dawn reluctantly
> Left Tithonus in her rose-shadowed bed.
> Then shook the morning into flakes of fire.

I love 'rose-shadowed' and 'flakes of fire', although they are not in Homer at all. Lombardo stylishly stole them from Tennyson's great poem, 'Tithonus', which has 'rosy shadows' and the marvellous line, 'beat the twilight into flakes of fire'. These moves – like Lombardo's playful quotation from Nabokov at the start of his *Odyssey* – raise interesting questions about what counts as a 'translation', as opposed to a fun reinvention inspired both by the original and various other somewhat related texts. It is also notable that Lombardo adds 'reluctantly' (corresponding to nothing in the Greek): in this version, poor Tithonus has no epithet and is only good for one thing. Lombardo makes Dawn a working lady, who finds it challenging to juggle her enjoyable sex life with her career responsibilities. The focus on mortality and immortality, and the various parallels between Dawn, Calypso and Hermes are eliminated in the translation.

This is my own version of these same lines:

> Then Dawn rose up from bed with Lord Tithonus,
> to bring the light to deathless gods and mortals.

As you can see from these examples, mine is the only modern one that has regular metre, using traditional iambic pentameter. I want to try to 'translate' the traditional poetic form of the original, in dactylic hexameter, by using its equivalent in English, the metre most associated with narrative verse in our literary heritage.

I spent many hours considering what to do with the purpose clause. I liked the almost-suggestion that Dawn is like a mail-woman, bringing the daily necessities to diverse populations – I wondered if some readers might hear, as I do, a buried echo of Larkin's 'Aubade'. But here as elsewhere, I wanted to avoid the clever literary allusions of Lombardo or Fitzgerald, since they are entirely out of place in Homeric poetics; the *Odyssey* is based on a pre-existing oral tradition, and cannot make smart little nods to earlier literature, because there was no earlier Greek literature.

The relative starkness of my version, compared to some of the more expansive translations, is deliberate. I tried, here and elsewhere, to avoid spelling out things that are resonantly unspoken in the original – such as to whom the bed belongs, and whether Dawn is glad or sorry to be getting up. The reader or listener has the right to dwell in ambiguities, when the original is meaningfully ambiguous, rather than having everything explained and glossed by the translator. One detail is to me an essential feature of the original Greek: that the 'deathless' and the 'mortals' are not linguistically or metaphysically alike. For that reason, I chose words from two different linguistic roots ('deathless' and 'mortals', rather than 'immortal/mortal'), in contrast to many other translators, who bring the two categories closer together. I regretted not managing to do more alliteration, to reflect that of the original (*phoōs pheroi*), beyond the repeated 'to'. I alliterate elsewhere, not always in the same places as the original, because it's not always possible without adding elements that are pure invention (as Lombardo and Pope do).

How can a translator bring the light from ancient Greece to modernity? What does she bring with her, and what does she leave behind? For whom is the light shed? I hope this little exercise helps illustrate some of the many dilemmas, and the eternal, deathless, immortal fact that there is no one true right answer.

Implicit in many of these translation choices are various

assumptions that translators bring from their own time period, including ideas about proper gender roles and sexuality, beliefs about labour and enlightenment, and changing literary norms about what makes a text sound 'poetic'. The Homeric poems, like all ancient poetry, do not rhyme; and yet, in Chapman or Pope's times, rhyme was a normal element in contemporary poetry, and is therefore introduced. Similarly, unmetrical free verse did not exist in antiquity, but twentieth-century translators often use it because it is a normal poetic form to contemporary readers. Grand vocabulary words and archaisms are viewed as 'poetic' by many twentieth- and twenty-first-century readers, and so they make their way into translations of ancient poetry – regardless of the lexical register of the original.

Modern popular reception of ancient poems can also shape modern translations, even when there is a clear gap between the ancient text and later reinventions of the story. One example is the story of the Sirens from the *Odyssey*, the divine female singers who tempt all those who sail past to listen to them forever, forgetful of their families. Odysseus, instructed by Circe, has himself bound to the mast so he can listen to their song. He also has his men bung up their ears with wax so they cannot hear and be tempted. In the modern popular imagination, the Sirens are tempting because they are sexy mermaid-like ladies, as in the Siren scene in the Coen brothers film, *O Brother Where Art Thou*. From a modern perspective, the Homeric Sirens passage is surprising in at least two ways. One is how short it is; the episode has become a much bigger part of the *Odyssey* in modern retellings than it is in the Homeric original. Secondly, the Sirens in Homer are not sexy. The modern visual iconography of Sirens as scantily clad mermaids is very different from ancient depictions (vases, mosaics etc.), which make them bird-women-poets; they often have musical instruments, the lyre and/or the aulos (double pipe), and offer a musical, aesthetic temptation, and a cognitive one: they promise to enable knowledge. In the Homeric text, we learn nothing even about their hair or ankles, in contrast to other divine temptresses in archaic Greek poetry. This fits with the visual iconographic tradition, in which Sirens often have bird legs and claws: the avian tarsometatarsus is not usually desirable to a human gaze. The seduction Sirens offer is based on their claim to know everything about the war in Troy, and everything on earth. They tell the names of pain. But there is a tendency among translators to fight back against these facts about the original text – perhaps not always consciously.

Here are three lines from the passage, in which the Sirens tell Odysseus he should stop and listen to them, as so many have done before:

> οὐ γάρ πώ τις τῇδε παρήλασε νηὶ μελαίνῃ,
> πρίν γ᾽ ἡμέων μελίγηρυν ἀπὸ στομάτων ὄπ᾽ ἀκοῦσαι,
> ἀλλ᾽ ὅ γε τερψάμενος νεῖται καὶ πλείονα εἰδώς.

The Loeb prose translation reads, 'For never yet has any man rowed past the island in his black ship until he has heard the sweet voice from our lips; instead, he has joy of it, and goes his way a wiser man.' The Greek word *stoma* means 'mouth'; and yet this translation renders it as 'lips'. It is, of course, possible to argue that English speakers are more likely to think of speech as emerging from the lips rather than the mouth. But the translation of mouth as 'lips' also fits in nicely with the modern perception of the Sirens as seductive, rather than cognitively tempting – especially when *tis*, the unnamed 'someone' who passes by in a black ship, is translated in emphatically gendered terms, as a 'man'. 'Man' is repeated twice in the Loeb translation, and is not paralleled by a gendered noun in the Greek – although the traveller is implicitly male.

Modern anglophone translators seem to have been quite consistent in rendering the *stomatōn* of the Sirens as 'lips', and often add 'man' once or twice. Lattimore does the same thing: 'the honey-sweet voice that issues from our lips'. Fagles, often an expansive translator, has 'the honeyed voices pouring from our lips'. Lombardo also has lips, and turns the Sirens' voice (*ops*) into the dehumanised 'sound', as if these goddesses were a strange and rather sticky kind of music machine: 'listening to the honeyed sound from our lips'.

Of those I have looked at, the translator who does most to impose modern sexy mermaids onto the Homeric bird-like Sirens is Fitzgerald. He shifts to a different metre for their song, using italics and lovely ballad-like rhyming stanzas, and expanding so radically that three lines of Greek become thirteen in the translation:

Sweet coupled airs we sing.
No lonely seafarer
Holds clear of entering
Our green mirror.

Pleased by each purling note
Like honey twining
From her throat and my throat,
Who lies a-pining?

Sea rovers here take joy
Voyaging onward,
As from our song of Troy
Greybeard and rower-boy
Goeth more learnèd.

Some details of the translator's additions evoke Shakespeare, especially *The Tempest* ('green mirror', 'coupled airs'); the passage would seem at home in Auden's long poetic riff on *The Tempest*, 'The Sea and the Mirror'. Some are more generically ballad-like or early modern ('greybeard', 'a-pining'). Several of the additions make the Sirens seem much more seductive, in the traditional, 'feminine wiles' manner, than the original does: these Sirens have not mouths but 'throats', and their song seems designed to wind itself around the unsuspecting male traveller, 'twining' and 'purling'.

In my own translation of this passage, I translate *stomatōn* literally as 'mouths'.

> 'Now stop your ship and listen to our voices.
> All those who pass this way hear honeyed song
> poured from our mouths. The music brings them joy,
> and they go on their way with greater knowledge.'

I wanted to match in my translation the impression that I see in the Greek: the Sirens are seductive, but in aural, musical and intellectual ways, not because they are sexy mermaids. I tried to echo some of the alliterating sibilants in the original, a bit like Kaa in *The Jungle Book*. I also felt that the literal rendition of 'mouths' was important, even if English idiom could accommodate 'lips', because it is the mouth, not the lips, that run through the poem's central preoccupation with the themes of eating and being eaten. Mouths (of giants, goddesses, men, the sea itself) keep eating the wrong things, and mouths (of goddesses, men, witches, singers and shades) speak and sing to enable or thwart the onward journey. Unlike lips, which can be pretty and kissable, mouths are powerful and dangerous.

Perhaps the trope of kissable Sirens is a specifically modern interpretation. It is not legible in pre-twentieth-century translations. Chapman includes no lips, and focuses on cognitive ravishment rather than the other kind: his Sirens tell 'Ulysses' to 'that song hear / That none past ever but it bent his ear, / But left him ravish'd, and instructed more / By us, than any ever heard before'. Similarly, Pope makes them offer quasi-spiritual enlightenment, and makes no mention of either lips or mouths: 'Blest is the man ordain'd our voice to hear, / The song instructs the soul, and charms the ear'. The alluring mermaid became much more of a cultural touchstone during the nineteenth and twentieth centuries, with the rise in popularity of the 'Little Mermaid' and its various cinematic adaptations, and with the fusion of Scandinavian folk traditions of seductive sea-women with the ancient Siren myth. The phrases 'siren song' and 'femme fatale' have become much more common in English over the past eighty years. The common modern image of the sexy, seductive siren may seem 'traditional', and in a sense, it is – but traditions are often much more recent than we think.

The intertwining of modern values and prejudices with the translation of ancient texts affects many features of translation that have nothing to do with gender. One example is a passage of Book 9 of the *Odyssey*, in which Odysseus and his men encounter a huge, wild man – a Cyclops. In modern popular imagination, the Cyclops is a 'monster', who is often imagined as a dehumanised 'savage', a term associated with modern European and anglophone racialised stereotypes about other parts of the world. And yet in the Greek, Polyphemus is a human being, and the son of a god – although he is also strange to his Ithacan visitors in his habits and his physical appearance, and responds poorly to the appearance of uninvited guests, whom he swallows for dinner. He is terrifying, but he is not a different species from Odysseus – and in some ways, as the son of a god, he is superior rather than inferior to his visitors. Translators sometimes iron out this complexity by presenting Polyphemus as inhuman. We can see these tendencies in the translation of just a couple of lines. When Odysseus and his gang have blinded the Cyclops and snuck out of his cave, clinging to the bellies of the shepherd's rams, they row away at top speed. But Odysseus can't resist taunting his blinded victim. The men try to restrain him, with these words:

σχέτλιε, τίπτ' ἐθέλεις ἐρεθιζέμεν ἄγριον ἄνδρα;

Here, the men criticise Odysseus with a word suggesting 'cruel' or 'unflinching' or 'stubborn' – a word that Odysseus had earlier used to the Cyclops – and define the Cyclops explicitly as a human being, a man: *andra* is the same word used of Odysseus himself in line 1 of the poem. Polyphemus is defined as a country-dwelling or wild man (*agrion*). But he is definitely a person.

And yet several translations apply the word 'man' to Odysseus, but not to Polyphemus. The Loeb translation has, 'Stubborn man, why will you provoke to anger a savage?' Fitzgerald makes the men address Odysseus with an honourable title (not a term of criticism), and call Polyphemus not a man but a 'beast': 'Godsake, Captain! / Why bait the beast again?' Lombardo, as he does quite often, leaves most of this line out, and, like the Loeb, makes Odysseus the 'man', not the Cyclops. His rendition is simply, 'Don't do it, man!' Fagles quotes Fitzgerald (as he frequently does), using 'beast': 'So headstrong – why? Why rile the beast again?'

In my own translation, I wanted it to be clear, as it is in the Greek, that the Cyclops is defined as a human being. I render the line, 'Calm down! Why are you being so insistent / on taunting this wild man?' I used 'wild', which I felt captured something of how the Greek word hovers between neutral description (wild animals aren't worse than tame ones) and judgement.

Translations are informed by, and inform, scholarly discourse as well as current popular receptions. The 'savage', 'monster' and 'beast' renditions are paralleled by the Oxford commentary by Albert Heubeck, which notes of the Cyclops people: 'this race [*sic*], the embodiment of inhumanity, is endowed with non-human characteristics and is capable of acts of extreme barbarity.' The notion of Polyphemus as 'inhuman' is both standard and highly debatable.

Grafting contemporary values onto ancient texts is, presumably, often done unconsciously. It is very rare for a translator to deliberately set out to distort the original she or he is translating. It can be as difficult for us to see the cultural assumptions of our own time as for a bird to see air, or fish water. For instance, in renditions of the violent scene in *Odyssey* book 22, in which Telemachus kills the thirteen enslaved people who have served the bodily desires of Penelope's suitors, modern assumptions about sex and gender are often very clear in the translator's choice of phrase.

After Odysseus has slaughtered the suitors who have been harassing his wife, he delegates the final set of killings to his son, Telemachus. These last victims are very different from those Odysseus himself kills: they are not armed young men, but unarmed enslaved people – the twelve women who have shared the suitors' beds, and the one man who has brought them animals to eat. These thirteen people have been claimed by alternative owners, whom they remember, and they are therefore a threat to the ultimate goal of Odysseus's homecoming, his *nostos*: to regain full control and honour in the house. The point is not that they must be punished because they have committed crimes or sins, out of their own lust or greed and through their own agency, but that, willingly or unwillingly, they have been used for the lust and greed of men other than Odysseus. Their continued existence therefore undermines his honour and that of Telemachus and Penelope. Odysseus instructs his son to hack the life out of them with long swords. Telemachus adjusts the weapon: he insists they are too metaphorically dirty to touch with his sword, so he hangs them instead. The rope round the throat provides the ideal way to stop a woman's most threatening orifice, her mouth.

Before the killings, Telemachus insists that these enslaved people cannot have a 'clean' death, because they 'poured' shame on himself and his mother:

> μὴ μὲν δὴ καθαρῷ θανάτῳ ἀπὸ θυμὸν ἑλοίμην
> τάων, αἳ δὴ ἐμῇ κεφαλῇ κατ' ὀνείδεα χεῦαν
> μητέρι θ' ἡμετέρῃ παρά τε μνηστῆρσιν ἴαυον.

The women are described simply with a pronoun, *taōn* ('of them', feminine plural). There is no noun, and Telemachus does not level any term of abuse at them, beyond describing them as bringing shame. There is no way to tell whether Telemachus agrees with his father's earlier claim, that the women were 'forced' into sex with the suitors ('biaiōs', 'forcibly', 22.38) – and, from the perspective of honour, it is irrelevant: they may have had little or no choice, but, nonetheless, they must die. Telemachus is ashamed and disgusted by the existence of women whose bodies have been claimed by other men. Moreover, the social world of the Homeric warrior entails a focus on honour that is, in the domestic sphere, dependent on complete control of the bodies within the household, including the wife and the enslaved members of the estate. A man whose wife and/or slaves have been claimed by others is thereby humiliated, whether or not they wanted to be so claimed.

And yet many translations have him use lively terms of abuse in this passage, as if Telemachus were not performing an honour killing, but was instead punishing sexual miscreants. In Fagles' bestselling version, Telemachus addresses them as 'You sluts – the suitors' whores!' Lombardo draws from Fagles: 'sluts'. Lattimore uses 'creatures'. Fitzgerald uses 'sluts'. The version by Alexander Pope has the liveliest term of abuse: he calls them 'nightly prostitutes to shame' (a vivid image that corresponds to nothing in the Greek).

One might be tempted to think that the sexualised condemnation of these murdered women by male translators was an inevitable result of the translators' gender. But this notion fails to fit the evidence. The Anne Dacier version in French prose was the first known complete published translation by a woman (1716), and Dacier suggests an active plot to sow disorder in the bourgeois home on the part of these messy, nasty girls:

> Il ne faut point faire finir par une mort honorable des créatures qui nous ont couverts d'opprobre ma mère et moi par la vie infame qu'elles ont menée, et par tous les désordres qu'elles ont commis.
>
> [One must not make the end of an honourable death for creatures who have covered my mother and myself with shame by the life of infamy they led, and by all the disturbances they created.]

The word '*créatures*' dehumanises the victims, and instead of the neutral description of behaviour (they 'lay beside' the suitors, *para te mnēstērsin iauon*), the women are said to have led a 'life of infamy', *la vie infame*, and created a lack of order in the household (*désordres*). Dacier was a pioneering translator, who fought hard against the 'pretty little liars' perception of poetic translation popular in her time (more artful translations were known as *les belle infidèles*). Against the elegant, metrical, rhyming versions of her peers, she reimagined Homeric poetry in sturdy French prose, presenting the ancient epic in a way that could shore up good Christian, French values, and address the servant problem at the same time. It is likely that Pope's moralising against the 'prostitutes of shame' is motivated not so much by his gender identity as by his sources: his Greek was shaky, and he used Dacier extensively.

Why do so many translators and scholars, both male and female, choose to put terms of abuse into the mouth of Telemachus, and present the killing as motivated by righteous rage, not shame? One possible answer is that this interpretation fits better with modern social norms and assumptions. A modern writer might assume that Telemachus would lose all sympathy from the reader if the killings were not seen to be motivated by something very bad that the victims had done. Killing to defend one's honour is not normally considered appropriate in modern societies. Perhaps, too, modern forms of misogyny tend to focus directly on women's sexuality rather than on the dangers they may pose to the household and the honour of the male householder. A final reason, perhaps the most important, is entropy: once one translation has a sexualised term of abuse, others follow – regardless of whether it parallels or makes sense of the Greek.

This same passage provides an opportunity to examine how a translator might – by accident or design – cut complexities from a passage that might represent more than one point of view. Homeric scholarship over the past couple of decades has moved towards a much more nuanced and detailed recognition of how perspective shifts around in Homer, and how rarely we are limited to only one character's feelings or experiences. On the battlefield, we see both the killers and the killed; and here too, in the killings within Odysseus's house, we can hear both the perspective of the killer – the fragile young person eager to prove himself as a man, and to slough off the burden of many years of humiliation and of being bullied in his own home – and the perspective of those killed, who want to go home, to bed, and who do not want to die. And yet many English translations limit the perspective, so that the narrative seems to be focused largely or entirely on the eyes of the killer, not the victims.

A great Homeric simile describes the women's death. They are like birds, trying to fly, who are trapped in a net. One can take this simile as a mark of the narrator's broad sympathies, which include pity for those killed so that the protagonist can regain his full renown. One man gets his successful journey home from war, his *nostos*. This word, from which we get 'nostalgia' (the pain of never getting back to the past), suggests a physical journey. But the *Odyssey* reminds us that homecoming may be more than a geographical process. It also entails the rebuilding and destruction of relationships and of memories, both of which are essential to the construction of a household as a generator of honour for its master. For Odysseus to regain his glorious identity as lord of Ithaca and owner of his household and estate, others – like these birds, flying to their homes and ending up in a net, or these women, whose throats are silenced by the rope, whose feet are immobilised by the drop – will never go anywhere again. Their dream to achieve a *nostos* will never be fulfilled.

Alternatively, one could take it that the simile serves primarily to dehumanise the victims: perhaps they are compared to birds to reduce our sympathy, because nobody really cares about birds. In translation, just as in criticism or commentary or teaching, there are interpretative choices and forks in the path. Most of the translations I have looked at seem to take the second path, although to me, the first makes better sense of the Greek, and fits better with the breadth of Homeric vision – the ability of these epics to invite us to see more than one point of view, even or especially in scenes of violence and dominance.

Here is the simile in Greek:

> ὡς δ' ὅτ' ἂν ἢ κίχλαι τανυσίπτεροι ἠὲ πέλειαι
> ἕρκει ἐνιπλήξωσι, τό θ' ἑστήκῃ ἐνὶ θάμνῳ,
> αὖλιν ἐσιέμεναι, στυγερὸς δ' ὑπεδέξατο κοῖτος,
> ὣς αἵ γ' ἑξείης κεφαλὰς ἔχον, ἀμφὶ δὲ πάσαις
> δειρῇσι βρόχοι ἦσαν, ὅπως οἴκτιστα θάνοιεν.
> ἤσπαιρον δὲ πόδεσσι μίνυνθά περ οὔ τι μάλα δήν.

In his rendition, Chapman makes it unambiguous that these are wicked women by adding the biblical image of the sinner as 'stubborn-necked': the rope is put around the women,

> Till euery one
> Her pliant halter, had enforc't vpon
> Her stubborne necke.

The Greek has no 'stubborn', and Chapman omits the Homeric narrator's final evocation of pity as the proper response to these violent deaths (*oiktista*).

The women's feet twitch in their death throes. Pope skips the feet and their final movement, and adds a quasi-Christian set of souls, which are clearly going you-know-where:

Soon fled the soul impure, and left behind
The empty corse to waver with the wind.

These choices might seem to illustrate the religious and gendered norms of the earlier translators' benighted times. But the tendency to dehumanise the victims, and to blame them for their own deaths, is also present in twentieth- and twenty-first-century versions, although none of the modern translations are as explicitly Christianising as Chapman or Pope. The Loeb version of the simile reads,

as when long-winged thrushes or doves fall into a snare that is set in a thicket, as they seek to reach their roosting place, and hateful is the bed that gives them welcome, even so the women held their heads in a row, and round the necks of all nooses were laid.

'Held their heads' suggests that they are willingly submitting to this natural process; the very common, relatively unmarked verb *echon* could suggest either 'hold' or 'have', but the Loeb translators choose to make the victims collude with their death.

Robert Fitzgerald makes the women even more eager to die:

like doves or larks in springes triggered in a thicket,
where the birds think to rest – a cruel nesting.
So now in turn each woman thrust her head
into a noose and swung, yanked high in air,

to perish there most piteously.
Their feet danced for a little, but not long.

'Thrust her head' suggests that the women are longing, perhaps even lusting, for death. The suggestions of sexualised promiscuity are underlined by Fitzgerald's characteristic use of artful literary allusion: 'springes' recalls Polonius warning Ophelia not to let Hamlet take her virginity, telling her that the seductive words of young men are 'springes to catch woodcocks'. Implicitly, the translation presents these young women as a dozen fallen Ophelias, who have yielded to illicit sexual impulses – and have, like Ophelia, killed themselves. The final movement of their suspended feet (*ēspairon* – a word used almost exclusively for the last twitching movements or gasps of the dying) becomes, with a new metaphor invented by Fitzgerald, a dance; there is a clear connection between the bad kind of fun the women have enjoyed in life, and their suspended deaths.

Fagles borrows the word 'yanked' from Fitzgerald, although it corresponds to nothing in the Greek, and he recalls the earlier translators' image of these victims as party girls:

Then, as doves or thrushes beating their spread wings
against some snare rigged up in thickets –
flying in for a cozy nest but a grisly bed receives
  them –
so the women's heads were trapped in a line
nooses yanking their necks up, one by one,

so all might die a pitiful, ghastly death …
They kicked up heels for a little – not for long.

Where Fitzgerald makes Homeric poetry sound densely literary, with the Shakespearean allusion and the slight archaisms ('piteously'), Fagles makes it veer between chattiness and melodrama. The childish half-rhyme, 'cozy … grisly' points to the horrorific mismatch between the women's desires and their deaths – but also encourages us not to take their experiences too seriously. Fagles presents these 'sluts' (his choice of words) as girls who have partied too hard. They are hung 'in a line', like chorus dancers or clubbers on a night out.

Lombardo takes a somewhat different approach to the dying movements. His norm is to offset all Homeric similes with italics, so the birds exist in a different typographic mode from the women:

Long-winged thrushes, or doves, making their way
To their roosts, fall into a snare set in a thicket,
And the bed that receives them is far from welcome.

So too these women, their heads hanging in a row,
The cable looped around each of their necks.
It was a most piteous death. Their feet fluttered
For a little while, but not for long.

The translation suggests that even at the moment of their deaths, the women are still like birds, fluttering – they are dehumanised in their last moments. 'Roosts' makes the birds' home definitely non-human, although the Greek term *aulis* is used to describe human encampments or tents. The archaism 'piteous' creates distance: from afar, we can observe that something painful is happening to someone else, but we don't need to feel it ourselves.

In my own translation of this passage (current version, slightly revised from the first published version), I wanted to reflect what I see in the Greek, which is a simile that increases rather than decreases our sense of pity at the deaths of these women – who wanted only what Odysseus himself wants, to go home and go to bed.

> As doves or thrushes spread their wings to fly
> home to their nests, but someone sets a trap –
> they crash into a net, a bitter bedtime –
> just so the women, heads all in a row,
> were strung up with the noose around their necks
> to make their death most pitiful. They gasped,
> feet twitching for a while, but not for long.

The violence of the Greek passage, as I read it, is presented with understanding and compassion both for the killer and for those he kills. Their final movements are not joyful, and they do not want to die. The narrator explicitly invites our pity for them. The simile reminds us that the homecoming of Odysseus means that many others will never get to go back to their homes.

The poem does not condemn the killings. Nor does it

endorse them. The narrator characteristically shows us multiple different perspectives on the action. Odysseus and Telemachus view these killings as necessary to restore their honour, and Athena, the divine lover of spoils, delights in their bloody triumph. But we are also shown what it feels like for the women, with their hopes of life and homecoming ended, like their lives.

As a final example, let's look at the opening lines of the poem, known as the proem. This passage is one of the most challenging for the translator, not least because it is one of the most iconic passages of ancient literature. It sets a tone, a mood – and yet it is also different in style from much of the poem, with its long, meandering sentence structure and its allusive references to parts of the story to come.

> ἄνδρα μοι ἔννεπε, μοῦσα, πολύτροπον, ὃς μάλα πολλὰ
> πλάγχθη, ἐπεὶ Τροίης ἱερὸν πτολίεθρον ἔπερσεν·
> πολλῶν δ᾽ ἀνθρώπων ἴδεν ἄστεα καὶ νόον ἔγνω,
> πολλὰ δ᾽ ὅ γ᾽ ἐν πόντῳ πάθεν ἄλγεα ὃν κατὰ θυμόν,
> ἀρνύμενος ἥν τε ψυχὴν καὶ νόστον ἑταίρων.
> ἀλλ᾽ οὐδ᾽ ὣς ἑτάρους ἐρρύσατο, ἱέμενός περ·
> αὐτῶν γὰρ σφετέρῃσιν ἀτασθαλίῃσιν ὄλοντο,
> νήπιοι, οἳ κατὰ βοῦς Ὑπερίονος Ἠελίοιο
> ἤσθιον· αὐτὰρ ὁ τοῖσιν ἀφείλετο νόστιμον ἦμαρ.
> τῶν ἁμόθεν γε, θεά, θύγατερ Διός, εἰπὲ καὶ ἡμῖν.

I'll comment here on some of the most widely read modern translations of this passage. First, the version by E. V. Rieu, revised by Peter Jones (1946/1991), which is still commonly read in the UK, although it is less popular in the US, where free verse translations are dominant.

> Tell me, Muse, the story of that resourceful man who was driven to wander far and wide after he had sacked the holy citadel of Troy. He saw the cities of many people and he learnt their ways. He suffered great anguish on the high seas in his struggles to preserve his life and bring his comrades home. But he failed to save those comrades, in spite of all his efforts. It was their own transgression that brought them to their doom, for in their folly they devoured the oxen of Hyperion the Sun-god and he saw to it that they would never return. Tell us this story, goddess daughter of Zeus, beginning at whatever point you will.

I quite like 'resourceful' for *polytropon* (from *polytropos*), although it conveys nothing of the original's implicit metaphors of turning and being turned; it would work far better if the epithet in the original had been *polymēchanos*. In some places, the translation is very expansive: for instance, the original has just three words for Odysseus's wanderings – *mala polla plagthē* – where Rieu has eight: 'was driven to wander far and wide'. The addition of 'was driven' removes an important ambiguity in the original: did Odysseus have any choice about his wanderings? The 'high seas' give a rollicking sense of adventure, although the original has no modifier for the sea. Rieu's prose characteristically uses a number of wordy phrases and abstract nouns where the original has finite verbs and participles: for instance, 'in his struggles' translates a participle (*arnumenos*) as does 'in spite of all his efforts' (*hiemenos*). In the Greek, the men straight up 'died' (*olonto* – a very common word for dying), while in this translation, their transgression 'brought them to their doom'. The effect is a more distanced, less direct narrative than the original. High, quasi-biblical diction ('anguish', 'doom', 'folly', 'transgression') sits a little uneasily with colloquial business-speak ('saw to it', 'whatever point').

Richmond Lattimore's version in free verse is even more verbose – far more so than the Greek.

> Tell me, Muse, of the man of many ways, who was driven
> far journeys, after he had sacked Troy's sacred citadel.
> Many were they whose cities he saw, whose minds he learned of,
> many the pains he suffered in his spirit on the wide sea,
> struggling for his own life and the homecoming of his companions.
> Even so he could not save his companions, hard though
> he strove to; they were destroyed by their own wild recklessness,
> fools, who devoured the oxen of Helios, the Sun God,
> and he took away the day of their homecoming.
> From some point

here, goddess, daughter of Zeus, speak, and begin
our story.

The seventy-four words of the original become 109 words in Lattimore – a fairly characteristic ratio of expansion. Lattimore's phrasing is often a long way from normal English, even when the original is quite ordinary within the idioms of Homeric Greek: no native English speaker, except a translator, would have written 'was driven / far journeys', or 'struggling for his own life'. Lattimore adds a noun, 'journeys', when there is none in the Greek, and like Rieu, he interprets *plagthē* to suggest that some external force has 'driven' Odysseus: the Greek verb is passive in form, but is typically used in the passive to mean 'wander' or 'drift'. Lattimore's protagonist is fundamentally inactive, and the translator undermines Odysseus's cognitive achievements as well: the Greek of *nöon egnō* suggests that he knew or understood the minds (or habits) of many people – but Lattimore's Odysseus only learns 'of' them, which doesn't indicate any particular intelligence. This translator, as is typical of his approach, adds repetitions where the original has none: here, for instance, there is the awkward repetition of 'of' with different senses and different stresses in the line ('of the man', 'of many ways', 'learned of'). The line breaks are markedly peculiar and off-putting; it is hard to understand, for instance, why Lattimore breaks the line at 'hard though', when the translation is using no metrical constraints and the Greek includes the whole participle phrase before the line break (*hiemenos per*). Lattimore skips

Hyperion, explains who Helios is, and adds 'wild' – choices that arguably make the men more idiotic, and their leader more caring, than they are in the Greek. The awkwardness of phrasing and the strange lack of fluency give a very different overall impression than does the vivid, rhythmical language of the original. And yet Lattimore's approach to translating Homer, in long, unmetrical, unidiomatic English lines, has been paralleled by numerous other late twentieth- and twenty-first-century translators, several of whom have differed mostly by being even more verbose.

Daniel Mendelsohn's 2025 translation begins, 'Tell me the tale of a man, Muse, who had so many roundabout ways / to wander, driven off course, after sacking Troy's hallowed keep.' Fourteen words in Greek have become twenty-four in English, through the addition of words and phrases that correspond to nothing specific in the Greek, though they often draw on the phrasing of earlier English translations: 'the tale' is an addition also found in the 1929 translation by Herbert Bates; 'off course' is a nautical phrase, not corresponding to anything in the Greek but also found in Robert Fagles' version, and in tune with the modern misperception of the poem's subject as a set of maritime misadventures; 'ways' expands the original epithet *polytropos* and is also found in the Loeb translation and Lattimore. Following Lattimore in his courageous defiance of contemporary English idiom, Mendelsohn presents Odysseus as if he were enduring a journey very much like driving through Milton Keynes – a nauseating and banal passage through one traffic circle after another.

The version by Robert Fitzgerald (1961) is far more elegant, and written in what is recognisably verse (using a largely iambic rhythm, although with many variations).

> Sing in me, Muse, and through me tell the story
> of that man skilled in all ways of contending,
> the wanderer, harried for years on end,
> after he plundered the stronghold
> on the proud height of Troy.
>   He saw the townlands
> and learned the minds of many distant men,
> and weathered many bitter nights and days
> in his deep heart at sea, while he fought only
> to save his life, to bring his shipmates home.
> But not by will nor valor could he save them,
> for their own recklessness destroyed them all –
> children and fools, they killed and feasted on
> the cattle of Lord Hêlios, the Sun,
> and he who moves all day through heaven
> took from their eyes the dawn of their return.
> Of these adventures, Muse, daughter of Zeus,
> tell us in our time, lift the great song again.

Many of the most charming details of this translation are entirely the invention of the translator, including the lovely 'in me ... through me', the 'story' (reflected by Mendelsohn's 'tale'), the 'dawn' of their return (rather than 'day'), the notion that Odysseus could not save the men 'by will nor valor', 'proud', 'distant', 'killed and',

'Lord', 'he who moves all day through heaven' (a wonderful addition), 'took from their eyes' (the Greek has nothing about blinding or sight), 'adventures' (a very modern idea of what the *Odyssey* is about), and 'lift the great song' – a beautiful echo of the Hebrew psalms, as translated in the King James Bible, imported into an entirely different ancient text. Fitzgerald is not afraid to use peculiar word choices, even when the Greek lexicon is very ordinary; for instance, the normal word for towns, *astea*, becomes 'townlands', and the vague statement that Odysseus suffered a great deal on the sea (*polla d'ho g'en pontōi pathen algea*) takes on new specificity in Fitzgerald: 'weathered many bitter nights and days'. The translation is very expansive, such that the two Greek words *andra … polytropon* are rendered by eleven English words: 'the story / of that man skilled in all ways of contending'. It is very hard to see how 'contending' can be got out of the Greek, although of course it does convey one of Odysseus's specialities. As English verse, I personally like Fitzgerald more than most of the modern British and American translations, because he is attuned to rhythm and the possibilities of the English language, in ways that many contemporary classicists are not. At the same time, the fine literary artifice – the clever, original phrasing and the dense allusions to earlier literature – are out of keeping with the oral poetics of the original.

The translation by Robert Fagles into free verse begins,

Sing to me of the man, Muse, the man of twists and turns…
driven time and again off course, once he had plundered
the hallowed heights of Troy.
Many cities of men he saw and learned their minds,
many pains he suffered, heartsick on the open sea,
fighting to save his life and bring his comrades home.
But he could not save them from disaster, hard as he strove –
the recklessness of their own ways destroyed them all,
the blind fools, they devoured the cattle of the Sun
and the Sungod blotted out the day of their return.
Launch out on his story, Muse, daughter of Zeus,
start from where you will – sing for our time too.

The Fagles translation is very loud, lively and chatty, so it is not surprising that it has remained a bestseller in the US. It makes Homer into easy reading. The translation is frequently far longer than the original, including repetitions where the original does not repeat ('the man … the man'), and often giving a little extra pep by adding contemporary American idioms and imagery that make this alien, very ancient poem feel familiar: 'twists and turns', 'time and again', 'off course', 'heartsick', and 'wiped out from sight' (borrowed from Fitzgerald). None of these images and phrases correspond to anything in the original. Fagles has a reputation for being a much looser translator than

Lattimore, and there are details here that might confirm this view: for instance, the Greek suggests 'cities of many men', not 'many cities of men'. More substantially – not necessarily wrongly – Fagles often amps up the emotional stakes, adding melodrama or sentimentality or intensity that is hard to find in the Greek. He uses 'devoured' as a translation for the normal word for 'eat' (*ēsthion*). Similarly, a favourite Fagles word is 'disaster', which corresponds here to nothing in the Greek but commonly recurs in his text: he constantly reminds us that the stakes are high. I like the use of 'sing' at the beginning and end of the passage, creating a nice ring composition – but the Greek *ennepe ... eipe* is a variation of two distinct cognate verbs, both of which suggest 'say', not 'sing', which is a different verb. 'Blind fools' introduces a metaphor that isn't in the Greek (*nēpioi* are 'fools' or 'childish', but not literally or metaphorically 'blind'), and again, Fagles' debt to Fitzgerald is clear. I like 'launch out' for the embarking of the poem, but it is entirely made up by Fagles (there is no ship metaphor in the original). More importantly, adding 'his story' for words that more literally suggest 'of these things' is a debatable choice: Fagles frames the whole poem as the story of a single individual, 'him', which the Greek does not do (and instead, the Greek shows us the intertwining of several distinct people's stories, and their varying degrees of success in finding and achieving their journeys home, their *nostoi*).

Finally, the Greek *kai hēmin* literally suggests 'also to us': Fagles has borrowed 'our time' from Fitzgerald. The borrowings of Fagles from Fitzgerald and Lattimore (and then of Lombardo from all three) are visible on every page, and are, of course, valid. There's no rule to forbid a retranslator from lifting a phrase from earlier translators. But these inheritances are worth noting, because if you have not read the original it may not be clear that these different translators are heavily dependent on each other, rather than each offering an independent interpretation of the original. And yet, despite Fagles' borrowing, the reading experience of the Fitzgerald and Fagles translations is very different. Fitzgerald's version is allusive and ornately literary, in a high modernist mode. Fagles is more grandiose, more Whitmanesque. In translating an ancient epic, he goes for intensity. The ellipses (...) are one of Fagles' favourite ways to build suspense – a typographical device that is, of course, alien to the original, which was experienced primarily in oral performance and written for many centuries with no punctuation at all, but which fits well with American late twentieth-century assumptions about what 'epic' poetry means.

Stanley Lombardo's slangy, unmetrical free verse translation borrows heavily from earlier American translations, especially Fagles. But it is one of the boldest in stripping out details from the Greek, and adding elements that are not, strictly speaking, paralleled by the original.

SPEAK, MEMORY –
Of the cunning hero,
The wanderer, blown off course time and again
After he plundered Troy's sacred heights.

Speak
Of all the cities he saw, the minds he grasped,
The suffering deep in his heart at sea
As he struggled to survive and bring his men home
But could not save them, hard as he tried –
The fools – destroyed by their own recklessness
When they ate the oxen of Hyperion, the Sun,
And that god snuffed out their day of return.
Of these things
Speak, Immortal One,
And tell the tale once more in our time.

The opening salvo, 'Speak, Memory', is a quotation from Nabokov (*Speak, Memory* is the title of the novelist's memoir) – inviting us to view the poem as a creative autobiography, presumably of Odysseus, who is, like the emigré Russian writer, much travelled and prone to self-reinvention. Word choices familiar from Fagles that do not correspond to the Greek are easy to spot, including 'off course' and 'hard'. Moreover, Lombardo draws on the imagery of Fagles in 'blotted out', slightly varying it as 'snuffed out' ('Out, brief candle!') – although no such imagery is there in the Greek. The grand 'Immortal One' is Lombardo's invention, and he characteristically omits several details from the Greek, including the fact that the goddess is a daughter of Zeus. His rendition of *polytropon* as 'cunning' is enticing, although it seems to be more an evocation of the general theme of the poem than a translation of this specific word: other Homeric epithets used for Odysseus, such as *polymētis* ('much-cunning') or *polymēchanos* ('much-devising' / 'much-problem-solve-y') would be better translations for the English word 'cunning'. The surprise of the Greek, in its use of an unusual descriptor for our familiar but ever-changing hero, is certainly not conveyed by Lombardo's predictably iconic choice of 'cunning' for the mythical smart guy.

Finally, here is my own current translation, revised since my published 2017 version.

Tell me about a complicated man,
Muse, who was lost so long and fled so far,
when he had sacked the sacred citadel
of Troy – and how he saw and understood
so many people and so many places,
and suffered so much in his heart at sea,
as he was struggling to save his life
and bring his men back home. But even so,
despite his efforts, he did not protect them.
Poor fools! They died by their own wilfulness –
they ate the cattle of Hyperion,
the Sun, who took away their chance of home.
Of these events now tell us also, goddess,
daughter of Zeus. Begin from anywhere.

I hoped to recreate certain alien features of the original that aren't reflected in most modern translations, including, most obviously, regular, traditional poetic metre. The original is dactylic hexameter, the traditional metre of narrative verse in archaic Greece, so – as noted earlier – I used the anglophone equivalent, iambic pentameter. I also wanted to recreate other poetic/sonic features of the original, such as alliteration (*polytropon ... polla ... plagthē, epei ptoliethron epersen / pollōn:* 'fled … far', 'sacked … sacred … so … suffered').

My aim, more broadly, was to evoke the energy and clarity and beauty and music and pacing of the original, avoiding both the flatness or awkwardness of the more 'literal' versions and the looser ones that tend to expand or riff on the original. I tried to think hard about how similar effects might be achieved by different linguistic means: it's impossible, for instance, to start an English sentence with the object ('man', *andra*), unless you repeat it (as Fagles does), but I wanted to avoid extra repetitions so I put 'man' in the emphatic position at the end of the line, rather than emphatically at the beginning, to try to create a similar effect. I tried in general to avoid adding extra metaphors or adorning the narrative with modern English idioms, as these other translators have done. My translation may seem stark, but that perception depends on a comparison with other translations rather than with the Greek.

And yet it is easy for anyone who has read the Greek, including me, to pick on features of my translation that are markedly different from the original – even beyond the fact that none of the words are the same. I found it impossible, for instance, to replicate the line breaks of the original, in moving from a metrical hexameter to a metrical pentameter: the Muse had to be deferred to the second line, although I hated to do it. In my revised translation, I tried even harder to reflect the original's emphasis on multiplicity (*polytropon ... polla ... pollōn ... polla*); but I remain not fully satisfied with my current solution, which entails repeating the adverbial 'so'. Translation, even more than most writing, takes dozens or hundreds of drafts, even when the translator has been reading the original text for decades before even beginning to consider how to English it. There's no such thing as 'the' right answer, and numerous different translations, including all of these, can provide valid but different portraits of the original. I hope my translations allow readers to engage in new ways with the complexities, humanity and depth of Homer.

As a final reflection on my own translation, let's look at just one word from this passage – the one over which many gallons of journalistic ink have been spilt: *polytropon* (from *polytropos*). Most Homeric characters have a small number of standard epithets, which can fit metrically with the name in different positions in the line. Achilles is 'swift-footed' and 'son of Peleus'. Agamemnon is 'lord of men' and 'son of Atreus'. Odysseus has more formulaic epithets than most, and a great many of them have to do with his multiplicity. He is a man of 'many strategems' (*polymēchanos*), 'much wiliness' (*polymētis*), 'much-enduring' (*polytlas*), 'much-smarts' (*polyphrōn*). He's also 'city-sacker' (*ptoliporthos*) – an epithet shared with several other warriors – 'resplendent/glorious' (*dios*), 'related to Zeus' (*diogenes*), 'godlike' (*theoeides*, *theoeikelos*), 'son of Laertes', and more.

So the poet of the *Odyssey* had a choice about how to describe the protagonist of the poem in the first line. Why choose a relatively unusual epithet, *polytropos* 'much-turny'? Why not choose one of those that focuses on Odysseus's intimacy with the gods, or one that focuses on his famous strategic intelligence, or his capacity for patience and endurance, all of which will be essential in the poem? These sets of epithets are far more common in the poem as a whole, but they are not what we get in line one.

I am very far from the first reader to think that the choice of this unusual epithet must be marked, and that it serves as a promise about the forthcoming poem as well as about the protagonist and his journey. This choice of epithet assures us that not only the man but also the epic itself will feature numerous twists and turns, and many contrasting, overlapping scenes of almost-homecoming, almost-arrival and almost-recognition, even after our hero comes back to Ithaca. Multiplicity, tricks and changes will be central to the story, and the first line hints at this enticing fact, while also – appropriately for the theme – keeping us in the dark about the specifics of these mysteriously, enticingly numerous narrative 'turns'.

In later Greek, the word can be applied to situations as well as to people, and it often seems to have negative connotations. Thucydides uses the word for multiplicity of situations in life, in the Periclean Funeral Oration (2.44): *en polytropois gar xumphorais epistantai traphentes* ('They know that they were brought up amid manifold circumstances'). It is used of a dangerously complicated or changeable disease (Plutarch, *Numa* 24: an evil king was cured of his impiety by a 'serious and complicated illness') and of war.

A rendering that could only apply to the man and not the poem or the trip did not seem adequate. A man can be 'crafty'. A poem or a journey can't. A trip or a poem (or a war, a disease or a circumstance) cannot be 'wily', which is a fine rendering of *polymētis*, but not of *polytropos*.

Polytropos isn't necessarily positive, at least in later uses. Plutarch applies it to the notorious turncoat, Alcibiades, in his biography of the same name. Plato's discussion of the relative moral merits of Homeric heroes (in *Hippias Minor* 364e) contrasts the 'very simple and very truthful' Achilles (*haploustatos kai alēthestatos*) with Odysseus as 'complicated', *polytropos*. Plato's usage suggests that to him, at least, *polytropos* definitely doesn't mean 'wise', because it is distinct from Nestor's quality of *sophia*. Of course, Plato was writing a good three centuries after the composition of the Homeric poems; there is no reason to assume that the values of later prose authors will be identical with those of the original *Odyssey*. But these later uses do give some inkling of how at least some ancient readers might have taken that epithet.

It's also important that *tropos* suggests way of life, custom, habit, guise, manner or character, as well as, literally, 'turn'. Arguably, the epithet anticipates the ways Odysseus will appear in many disguises, will tell numerous false autobiographies, and will succeed in code-switching, transforming himself to fit in with entirely different social worlds and environments with each island he visits. He can be and behave as many people, or nobody. This variability is an extraordinary and essential element of his heroic excellence, and it is not the same as his other extraordinary qualities. You could be great at solving problems and coming up with solutions to transform your environment for survival (*polymēchania*), as Odysseus does with the wooden horse, and with the raft on which he escapes the island of Calypso, and great at enduring against tough odds for a really long time without giving up (*polytlas*), without also being able to transform yourself into multiple guises and roles (*polytropia*). I needed to think through those connotations and distinctions to find the right word.

I was also keen to try to honour the pacing of the original. I confined myself to the same number of lines as the Greek. I did not want to produce a translation that was longer or wordier, or that risked being flabbier than the original. For that reason, I was reluctant to do what many translators have done: to render this single four-syllable word with a subordinate clause or a phrase, although I did play around with ways of doing it like that. 'A man who was turning and turned'. 'A man of many turns'. But those options have real costs, because the gripping pace and drive of the opening is lost as soon as you start shoving a many-word phrase into the first sentence. I wanted to translate a whole poetic and narrative experience, not write the explanatory footnotes as if they were the text. None of the options using explanatory phrases or clauses seemed to me to match the impact of the original, with the startling arrival of this powerful, unusual epithet in the middle of the line, after we've already had the noun. Moreover, 'a man of many turns' is more or less incomprehensible, certainly not vivid – and there is no reason to think that the original was difficult to understand. In English, 'turns' does not carry the connotations of many disguises or habits or characters. It is literal but unfaithful, in the sense that it doesn't make clear what is clear in the original. There's also potential for an unfortunate recollection of Austin Powers, International Man of Mystery. I also didn't want to introduce syntactical repetitiveness where the original is varied. I tried out, but then ruled out, many variations on 'a man who turned/was turned a lot, who also wandered a lot' – the original has only one relative clause and distinguishes between the primary quality of the *polytropia*, introduced in the main clause, and the subordinate clause account of the numerous wanderings.

I spent many hours, days and weeks searching around for alternatives. I eliminated 'twisty', which is great for an airport novel or a corkscrew, but not plausible for a person (and 'twisted' would be unfortunate, as would 'kinky' or 'perverted' – those are all the right metaphor, but the wrong connotations). 'Topsy-turvy' seems appropriate for a children's TV show, not an epic. 'Circuitous', or 'zigzag' or 'meandering' might work for a journey, but not so well for a person, and 'meandering', a lovely word, runs into the alliteration problem – there is already too much inevitable alliteration ('man ... me ... Muse'), which also rules out all cognates of 'movable' or 'mobile', which also fail to connote movement that's not straight; Odysseus's movements are far more varied. 'Flexible' suggests yoga. 'Turned' sounds like spoiled milk. 'Versatile' seemed like an option for a while, but it is boring and does not work well to connote the actual travel or the poetics of poem, as opposed to the character. And besides, 'a versatile man' does not scan in an iambic line, so it would have required some syntactical contortions ('a man of versatility' – a terrible, clunky mess).

It would be fun to use 'translated', like Shakespeare's Bottom. That would have made for a nice piece of homage to the Latin translator, Livius Andronicus, who used *versutus* for his mostly lost Latin verse translation of the *Odyssey*. I was tempted by that option for a while, because I liked the idea of those layers of allusion and homage, paralleling the metapoetic connotations of the original. But it would have been a solution that most readers would find more confusing than illuminating, and I did not want to suggest anywhere, let alone in the first line, that the *Odyssey* is a cleverly allusive, literary text. The Homeric poems are based on an oral tradition, they are not difficult Greek, and layered, self-consciously literary allusions, are completely alien to Homeric quasi-oral poetics. As a translator of Homer, it isn't my job to try to be clever. That was certainly part of my job as a translator of Euripides or Seneca, but not Homer. Homeric poetry needs to sound traditional and in a sense entirely artificial – hence my use of very regular and very traditional metre – but not allusive or markedly literary. I wanted the translation to be stylized, rhythmical and traditional in verse form, with some elements of grandeur or majesty, able to mutate for a range of different registers and moods, but also to feel fresh, as if it had sprung from the spoken language of the people, whatever that means in contemporary English. So, no 'translated', and nothing too fancy. It needs to be a real word, in regular speech – and yet somehow surprising.

So I went with 'complicated', which suggests something of the imagery (folding or layers, which are analogous to turns) and has the same syllable count as the original, and is a real, not made-up, English word, conveys immediate meaning, as the original does, but is appropriately multiple, and hints at truths to come, about the character, the poem and the trip. It is direct and comprehensible, as the original is, and it is also, like the original, an injunction to watch out for complexity in unexpected places. This word choice is potentially a shock, not quite what you expect at the start of an epic poem – which also feels right, given that the original is an unusual and surprising word choice.

I like the concept of complexity as a positive quality in the world of this poem and this protagonist, and for setting the mood for the rest of the poem and the translation. In teaching Homer to undergraduates I have seen that students frequently assume that very old poems will have simple morals, simple psychology, and simple heroes, regardless of the translation. I liked 'complicated' as a way of reminding the reader right away to reconsider that assumption. The word 'complicated' is itself ostensibly simple, like the narrative of the *Odyssey*, and like Homeric syntax, narrative and poetics. This poem tells a story of a man going home. But there are so many layers and disguises beneath.

I have sometimes been scolded for the choice of 'complicated'. Sometimes it's by people who have read only the first line, and none of the rest of the translation. Sometimes it's by people who say that they like everything about the translation except 'complicated'. Bless them.

I commonly hear two objections.

One is that some readers seem to think that it's negative, which is quite an odd response as far as I can see. The word does not, to my ear, have connotations that are either definitely positive or definitely negative. It's certainly less negative than other options, such as 'kinky' or 'turncoat'. There is nothing wrong with being complicated! We all are! I am, for sure, and I don't see it as a bad thing. It's far less negative than Plato's usage of *polytropos* would suggest – I would be more convinced by an argument that it's not negative enough. But I did not want to go all-out negative, because I don't think the original justifies that. Complexity, in a poem or narrative, or a mythical character, is surely all to the good. I see the original, and my translation, as a promise, or even an enticement: 'Dear Listener, stay with me, because you won't be bored by this character or this poem.' Who doesn't love disguises and schemes? Who doesn't love the tale of a long con? The narrator is promising us, implicitly, that we'll get an inside scoop on a character whose many layers, turns, names and disguises won't be visible to everyone he encounters. Uncomplicated characters are a hard sell, if you want the adult listener to stay with you for many hours of story. Complexity, sign me up. I am not the least bit original in seeing the Homeric Odysseus as a complex and multilayered character, who arouses our intense interest and intense empathy, and who is viewed in very different ways by different characters throughout the poem, because he contains multitudes. Homer's Odysseus is a distinct and far more appealing character than the often simpler and often more purely evil Odysseus we find in some other ancient sources (like the scheming sophist of Sophocles' *Philoctetes*, or the cruel Ulysses of the *Aeneid*). To me, 'complicated' does not suggest either 'good guy' or 'bad guy': it is rather a promise that this poem will not stoop to those implausible simplifications.

Some people seem to be very touchy about ancient characters. If people want 'heroes' who are entirely sympathetic, or ethically uncomplicated, and who would never let anyone die under their command, daytime soap operas may be a better bet than Homer.

The second issue for some readers is the idea that 'complicated' sounds 'too modern'. The word 'complicated' isn't particularly modern in English (*OED* cites 1656 as the first known instance of the modern meaning). But maybe 'complicated man' has been on the rise (Google Ngram tells me that that phrase, and 'complicated relationship', have risen in popularity since the turn of this century). Maybe for some people it has resonances of a relationship status on Facebook, or, better, Avril Lavigne. I like the Lavigne lyrics for 'Complicated' as a text with a kind of resonance with the *Odyssey*: 'acting like you're somebody else' is a central feature of Odysseus's *polytropia*, and it's essential to how and why he survives. If you do hear the song in the line, maybe it helps suggest the connotations of 'many guises' that are there in the original word. Sometimes you do have to make everything so complicated, sometimes you gotta wear your preppy clothes and strike a pose (or at least get your multiple goddess makeovers) if you want to survive as the warrior king of Ithaca.

For full disclosure: I tried to rewrite the whole passage at a very late stage, once I learned about the opening of the film *Shaft*, which I had not seen: the theme song by Isaac Hayes includes the line, 'He's a complicated man / but no one understands him but his woman.' I thought the possibility of that unintended allusion might mean that I had to throw out my draft. After weeks of attempting to rewrite, needing to rewrite everything else once that word was different, and making the whole proem flabbier, less vivid, more awkward, and all around worse every time, I realized that there was no better option – and that, actually, I quite like the *Shaft* intertext. Samuel L. Jackson would make a great Odysseus. The first line of the epic is not explicitly about the protagonist's complicated marriage, but that topic will prove essential in the poem to come.

I sometimes worry that 'complicated man' suggests something too internal, too psychological. But I also know that one can't avoid anachronistic connotations, in the inherently anachronistic process of translating from Homeric Greek to English, or indeed any modern language. It's a compromise, as is every translation choice ever. The question is how to choose the least bad compromise.

Is 'complicated' exactly the same as *polytropos*? No, of course not. Does it correspond in a lot of important ways, and perform many of the same functions in the sentence and the verse paragraph? Yes. Can I think of a way to improve on it? After many years of pondering the question, I'd still say: no.

If I live another twenty years, and retain the capacity to read, and if the world is still habitable by humans, I hope to see younger people come up with much better solutions than mine. I also suspect that we will have more important things to worry about by then.

AFTERWORD: TWENTY RULES

As a coda, I am presenting here a set of principles that guide many of my critical responses to retranslations of ancient literature, and that lie behind much of my own translation practices. I would also like to acknowledge that the practice of literary translation is never reducible to maxims: out in the wilds of words, the rules may clash with one another, and many a fine translator will find herself breaking some or all of these principles, in the eternal quest for fresh forms of equivalence.

1. If the original uses a traditional poetic verse form (or several such forms), the translation should find a way to honour this feature – for instance by using a traditional metre in the translation. What form feels 'traditional' will vary, depending on the traditions of the translator's language. Something important is lost if you render the regular traditional metrical verse of one language into prose or free verse in English.
2. It is a waste of everyone's time – the publishers, the translator, the potential readers – if a retranslation takes more or less the same approach as one or more

existing published translations. A retranslation needs to justify its existence by offering a new interpretation, just as a new critical monograph should do. Many retranslations of ancient texts do not have good reasons to exist, because they offer very little that differs from what came before. They may have been fun for the translator to produce, and they may make the publisher a few bucks if packaged well – but they are fundamentally pointless. There are dozens of possible valid ways to convey the stylistic features of a text in another language. Don't reinvent the wheel. Make it new.

3. Learn from experience about the needs of the reader. It's useful to have taught several different translations of the same canon to students over many decades, and to see what works and doesn't work in the classroom. Some translators and readers think the only way for a translation to be engaging for young readers is if it is full of predictable American slang or clichés. This is false. Everyone, including young people, deserves to learn new things.
4. Sometimes specific translation choices become entrenched, even among scholars or readers of the original – despite the fact that there is no such thing as 'the' translation. Try to rethink everything. Offer something different. It's OK to experiment. Turn things upside down. Reorient what's strange and what's familiar. Make room for surprises.
5. If every English translation of an ancient text is strange

or 'ancient-sounding' in the same old ways, Greekless or Latinless readers will not get a visceral sense of the specific strangeness of different ancient writers, nor understand that there are kinds of strangeness that go beyond syntax and word order. Ancient poets used their words to imagine and shape the narrative worlds they created, and we should exercise the same creativity in reconstructing their worlds.

6. Work with and against your readers' possible expectations. If readers may expect this text to be boring or archaic or simple-minded, and if those things aren't true of the original, think through how you can enable them to see something else.
7. If the original makes you laugh, cry, feel excited, get goosebumps, feel puzzled, get bored, be charmed, etc., then the translation should try to create those effects on its readers.
8. The translation should not feel slower or more boring than the original. Nor faster. Keep pace.
9. Be deliberate about what's difficult. If you're translating Sophocles, the imagery and double meaning should often feel riddling and enigmatic: the difficulty is essential to the poetic effect. If the original is clear to a fluent reader of the original, the translation should also be clear. This will take a great deal of work. Overwriting, muddle and clunk are very easy to achieve, as anyone who has graded student papers knows. Try harder.
10. Stylistic maximalism, poetic ornament, literary allusion and bombast are wonderful, at least sometimes. If

you're translating Seneca, you can pull out those stops. You can do it on your own time in non-translation poetry and fiction writing, if you want. But if the original text is grand or sublime or noble in a different way, the translation should consider alternative possible modes of grandeur. Milton is magnificent – but aiming for sub-Miltonic fireworks will not get you closer to the sound of Homer in English.

11. If the original has multiple characters or perspectives or voices, don't make them all sound the same.
12. If the original was designed for oral performance – as much of ancient poetry was, and much ancient prose – the translator should constantly read aloud the original and the draft in progress, and consider its effect on the ear as well as the eye. A clumsy phrase may look acceptable on the page, but the tongue reveals the truth.
13. If the original has moral or ideological tensions or complexities, those should be legible in the translation. All great works of literature have such complexities. Translate the ambiguities. Aim for negative capability. Don't join all the dots. Hope that future readers of your work may use it, reinvent it, push against it to create their own poems, plays, translations. Allow for more. Make room.
14. There are many sizes of infinity. There are an infinite number of ways to get a translation wrong. There are fewer ways to get it right – but the possibilities are still infinite. Don't stop experimenting. Don't give up too soon. There is always another way to say it.

15. Don't try to do it alone. Try out your drafts on readers of many kinds – those who have read the original, those who haven't, those who are experienced readers of poetry, those who aren't. Be humble enough to take their criticisms seriously.
16. Don't try to please everyone. If nobody objects to any choice you make, your choices are too timid.
17. If you're stuck, go for a walk. This applies to everything, not just translation.
18. Translation is reading, of the most intense kind. Read and reread the original until you're breathing it, tasting it, dreaming it. Even if you've been reading it for thirty years already, know how much there always is to see on each rereading. Be grateful that you get to be here with these texts every day.
19. Translation is writing, of the most intense kind. Your first draft will never be good enough. It takes many hours and some kind of magic to bring a text to life, whether it's a translation or an original poem. Stay with it, and maybe your thirtieth draft of the same few lines will start to breathe on its own.
20. Translation is difficult. This is not because it's difficult to read other languages. People who are bilingual aren't automatically brilliant literary translators. Rather, it's impossible to recreate every essential feature of a text – even the simplest and most boring of texts, let alone a whole magnificent ancient epic – in an entirely different language and cultural context. You will fail, of course. You will never be able to apply all your

principles successfully in every passage, line, word or syllable. But the project – of devoting your life to these great texts, of bringing them to life in new ways for new generations – is always worth it. Keep going.

ACKNOWLEDGEMENTS

Most of these essays would not exist without the initiative and labours of a wide array of brilliant editors. Being edited has made my writing and thinking immeasurably better. All remaining clunk is my own fault.

I owe a great debt to Jon Petre, the excellent editor at Profile Books, who provided insightful suggestions on the order of essays in this book and gave wise advice about the revision process. I am also grateful to Sam Kinchin-Smith, at the *London Review of Books*, for the initial idea of this book.

Thomas Jones at the *LRB* originally commissioned me to write on many of these topics. I have been repeatedly grateful for his editorial acumen, and I was also delighted to be able to collaborate with Tom on our *LRB* podcast series, 'Close Readings: The Ancients', which helped me develop new ways of introducing ancient authors to a general readership.

Other brilliant literary editors who have played an essential part in the genesis of these pieces include Mary Beard, Ian Buruma, Emmet Fraizer, Stuart Gillespie, David Marcus, Max Nelson, Adam Plunkett, Gemma Sack and Leon Wieseltier.

For support and patient toleration of my obsession with ancient literature and translation over the years, many thanks to my family, especially David Foreman. I have also been told to mention my cats, Pumpkin and Spice, so I do so, although in truth they have not helped at all.

Finally, I am truly grateful to have been sustained over the past couple of decades by the intellectual community here in the Department of Classical Studies at the University of Pennsylvania. Conversations with colleagues, graduate students and undergraduates over the years have repeatedly informed and shaped my approach to ancient literature, its receptions, and the challenges and possibilities of re-translation.

FURTHER READING

This is a list of some of the poets, authors and texts cited in this book.

Ancient texts, poets and authors

Note that many of the dates are debatable!

Aeschylus. Athenian tragic poet, 525–455 BCE. Extant plays include the *Oresteia* (a dramatic trilogy which itself includes *Agamemnon, Libation Bearers* and *Eumenides*).

Apuleius. African Roman writer and rhetorician, 124–175 CE. Author of *The Golden Ass*, also known as the *Metamorphoses*.

Aristophanes. Athenian comic poet, 446–386 BCE. Extant plays include *Frogs, Clouds, Acharnians*.

Catullus. Roman poet, 84–54 BCE.

Demosthenes. Athenian orator, 384–322 BCE.

Epictetus. Greek teacher of Stoic philosophy to mostly Roman elite students, 50–135 CE.

Euripides. Athenian tragic poet, 480–406 BCE. Extant plays include *Helen, Trojan Women, Medea* and many more.

Galen. Greek medical writer, 129–206 CE.

Herodotus. Greek historian/ethnographer, 484–425 BCE. *Histories.*

Hesiod. Archaic Greek poet, semi-legendary composer of *Theogony, Works and Days*, 600s BCE.

Homer. Archaic Greek poet, semi-legendary composer of *Iliad, Odyssey*, 600s BCE.

Livius Andronicus. Early Latin poet and translator, 284–204 BCE. Works are almost entirely lost.

Marcus Aurelius. Roman emperor, 121–180 BCE. Author of *Meditations*, jottings focused on self-improvement.

Menander. Greek poet of 'New Comedy', 342–290 BCE.

Ovid. Roman poet of love and change, 43 BCE–17 CE. Extant works include *Metamorphoses* and *Amores.*

Plato. Greek philosopher, 428–328 BCE. Extant works include *Republic, Symposium, Phaedrus, Phaedo, Apology of Socrates.*

Plautus. Roman comic verse dramatist, from 200s–100s BCE. Extant works include *Pseudolus.*

Plutarch. Greek biographer, essayist, philosopher, 40–125 CE.

Sappho. Greek female lyric poet who lived on the island of Lesbos, 500s BCE.

Seneca. Roman essayist, dramatist, philosopher, 4 BCE–65 CE. Extant works include *Letters to Lucilius* and tragedies including *Thyestes, Medea, Agamemnon, Oedipus.*

Simonides. Greek lyric poet, 555–565 BCE.

Sophocles. Greek tragic poet, 495–405 BCE. Extant works include *Oedipus Tyrannos, Antigone, Philoctetes, Ajax.*

Terence. Roman comic poet, 195–159 BCE. Extant works include *Mother-In-Law.*

Thucydides. Athenian military historian, 460–400 BCE. *History of the Peloponnesian War.*

Some modern translators/imitators

Samuel Butler, 1835–1902
Anne Carson, 1950–present
George Chapman, 1559–1634
Robert Fagles, 1933–2008
Robert Fitzgerald, 1910–1985
Richmond Lattimore, 1906–1984
Stanley Lombardo, 1943–present
Alexander Pope, 1688–1744
E. V. Rieu, 1887–1972
Sarah Ruden, 1962–present
Oliver Taplin, 1943–present

Other modern texts and authors

Walter Benjamin, 'The Task of the Translator' (1923)
Antoine Berman, *The Experience of the Foreign* (1992)
Ruby Blondell, *Helen of Troy* (2015)
E. R. Dodds, *The Greeks and the Irrational* (1951)
Denis Feeney, *Beyond Greek* (2016)

Edith Hamilton, *Mythology* (1942)
The Loeb Classical Library (1911 onwards)
Christopher Logue, *War Music* (2017)
Louis MacNeice, *Autumn Journal* (1939)
Madeline Miller, *Song of Achilles* (2011)
Jeffrey Henderson, *The Maculate Muse* (1975)
Friedrich Schleiermacher, 'On the Different Methods of Translating' (published posthumously, 1851)
Damion Searls, *The Philosophy of Translation* (2025)
Lawrence Venuti, *The Translator's Invisibility* (1995)

INDEX